Empowering YOU:
Let Go of the Past
&
Step Into YOUR Greatness!

Presented by Barbara H. Smith

Contents

III

Introduction

Have you ever experienced the suffocating grip of your past? That feeling of being unable to liberate yourself from the burden of a painful and traumatic history? Does the weight of past events continue to hinder your progress toward a brighter future? Do you yearn for a life untouched by the lingering ache of yesteryears? If these questions resonate with you, please understand that you are not alone. Many of us struggle with the challenge of letting go and moving forward.

But fear not, my dear friend, for there is indeed an escape. Within the remarkable pages of this book, you will be introduced to a group of extraordinary women who have triumphed over insurmountable challenges. They have confronted illness, fought valiantly against addiction, weathered the storms of devastating loss, and stood tall in the face of discrimination. Yet, they refused to let these trials define them. Instead, they summoned the inner strength to release the past and embrace their own greatness.

These remarkable women shine as beacons of inspiration, illuminating the path of possibility. They serve as living proof that no obstacle is insurmountable. Their presence is a gentle reminder, infused with boundless compassion, that you are never alone on your journey. Above all, they empower you to reclaim your innate power and author the life you truly yearn for.

Dear reader, this book is more than just a collection of stories. It's a heartfelt roadmap that will guide you toward a future filled with endless possibilities. It will gently show you how to break free from the chains of the past, allowing you to step into the radiant brilliance that resides within you. Together, let's embark on this transformative journey toward your greatness.

~ Barbara H. Smith

Dedication

This book is dedicated to:

- All those, men and women, who have felt trapped by their past, may these stories bring solace and strength to your heart.

- The remarkable women around the world who inspire us like guiding lights, they show us that no obstacle is too great to overcome. Their presence reminds us that we are never alone. Their compassion knows no bounds, offering support on our journey, with their empowering guidance, we reclaim our inner power, and author the life we yearn for, creating our own destiny.

May this book be a beacon of inspiration, a guiding light, leading you toward the limitless possibilities of your greatness.

~ Barbara H. Smith

Foreword

Letting Go of the Past and Stepping into Your Greatness

For many of us, our past is sprinkled with hardships, mistakes, and at times, a bad decision or two. We learn from them, grow from them, and move on to bigger and better things. We see it as a part of life's development process. At the same time, there are others who go through similar things but somehow become stuck in the process and are unable to move forward. For them, the past has become their prison and they are unable to move or advance.

Sometimes, others are stuck in the past not because of hardships and mistakes, but because they continually relive previous positive experiences, believing that their best years are behind them. They constantly retell the story of their athletic highlights, their college years, or maybe the romance that slipped away. Nostalgia has become their normal.

With both of these scenarios, the individual is often not aware that they are living life on pause. Some feel that their proximity to past hardships is what makes them a real warrior; therefore, they are unwilling to let go for fear of losing personal value. On the other hand, you have people who get an emotional rush every time they narrate the story of when they were on top of the world. They tell this same thirty-year-old story again and again, even to the same people.

The authors of this book have experienced some of these same scenarios. They have spent years emotionally wedged in the same place due to past experiences. They were filled with self-doubt, disbelief, guilt, and shame. All of which made them question whether they deserved to live life to the fullest. Fortunately, they were able to identify previous problems, become more self-aware, forgive themselves and others, and find the help they needed. Elevating their awareness was the key to initiating the change.

Now they have transparently come together disclosing real life struggles that most people cover up. They openly share the ups and downs, the highs and lows, as well as the good and the bad. Their goal is to help you understand that you are not alone when it comes to life's frustrations.

They are living examples of what life can look like when you let go of the past and focus forward. These writers divulge tips and strategies to overcome disasters and help you realign your life with your destiny.

We all have seen situations where the past has someone stuck on life's elevator. They are able to go up in some areas but never forward in others. They successfully get the next promotion or the next title, but on a personal level, there's no forward advancement. Or the person stuck on life's moving walkway. They are successful at moving forward but unsuccessful in elevating or progressing to the next level.

This book gives help to people in both of those scenarios. It provides a map of where you can go and a compass showing how to get there. It gives clear strategies on how to adjust your focus from the past to the future. How freeing would it be to release old grudges, reduce or eliminate fear, and embrace the necessary change for a new life? This book provides those strategies.

Reading, reviewing, and applying the strategies contained within this manuscript allows an individual to step off of the elevator and moving walkway and onto life's escalator where they can go forward and elevate to the next level at the same time. Get ready for a life changing experience. It's time to stop tripping over what's behind you, let go of the past, and step into your GREATNESS!

Ruben West, BCDPNP

Motherless Child

By Agnes Holmes

"I truly believe that the death of my mother has made me the way I am today. I am a survivor, mentally strong, determined, strong-willed, self-reliant, and independent."
— Hope Edelman

My father was a sharecropper, so I was born on a plantation in Branchville, Virginia. My mother and father had 17 children. I'm the youngest, now the only one still living. Alone... again. I only knew nine of my siblings because they were so much older. In addition, eight of them died at an early age. The other nine had families of their own, but we all lived on the plantation, just in separate houses.

When my mother was alive, everyone would come together to eat. Lunch and dinnertime were special. My mother would ring a bell loud enough to be heard across the fields, and all the family would stop working and come for lunch and/or dinner. It was a wonderful time. We always had a house full of family. I loved that then and now.

It was in elementary school that I started experiencing challenges. At that time, children started school in August when they were 6 years old. Since my birthday is in December, I missed the normal start to school in August. That meant I had to wait until the next school year to start the first grade, at those times there was no kindergarten.

1

By then, l was close to my 7th birthday. Starting late, and being tall for my age, always made me feel out of place. That meant I was not only older than all my classmates but taller as well.

I went to so many different schools because we moved so much. In one school I attended, all the students, no matter what grade, were in one single room. In another school, there were three classrooms for all grades. I think the reason we didn't require more rooms or teachers is because it was uncommon for there to be very many students attending school. Most students were out of school to work on farms unless it rained.

Just getting to the school was yet another challenge. We lived quite some distance from school. To get to school, we took a short cut through the plantation fields. Then, we travelled the path made by the horses and wagons. The woods were at the end of the path. We didn't take the main road because the white children rode buses to school and if we walked along the road, they would throw things or spit on us.

In November, right before my 8th birthday, my mother died. As a young child, I don't remember much about my mother or her passing away. I do have pictures of her with my father and memories of her that my family told me. Though she was absent, I always felt her presence with me.

One month after my mom died, my father remarried. I believe my father thought his new wife would help him with his two young children. When my dad remarried, my stepmother, let's call her Ms. P, wanted my father all to herself. That's when all my older brothers and sisters left the plantation and moved to different states. Me and my brother, James, were the only ones that remained and had to fend for ourselves.

At the end of that year, we moved to another farm that was not on a plantation. One of Ms. P's sons was now in charge of farming. Once Ms. P's son was in charge, we moved from farm to farm every two years. That also meant that every two years, I was changing schools. As soon as I got familiar with the school and my classmates, we were moving again. I never got into a routine, was confused not knowing where we would be next, and so it was difficult for me to adjust.

Ms. P had four sons, so she knew nothing about caring for a little girl like me. I was so tall that even my stepmother treated me like I was older than I was. She never cared for me, not even enough to comb my hair. She purposely had no time for me at all because she was active in multiple organizations.

She also loved to go fishing and stayed on the pond for hours. I didn't like fishing because I am afraid of worms and snakes. I am still afraid of snakes and worms to this day. So, while Ms. P went fishing, my brother and I were left alone at home all day. My father was always with Ms. P, either fishing or taking her to her organization meetings.

My life on the plantation was not easy. Even though we lived in a big house, there was no electricity, no running water, and no bathrooms. The living quarters were separate from the kitchen and dining area. At mealtime, to get to the eating area I had to go outdoors across a long porch to get to the dining room.

As a child, walking across the porch was very scary because no one was there to walk with me, I was a little girl... alone. My dad's new wife was not my mother, and she didn't know how to show me love.

Everything she said to me was negative and nasty. She would threaten me when she felt I wasn't moving fast enough and tell me that she was going to tell my dad on me. I thought to myself, "He's not your dad." When she was angry with me, she would make me stay in my room upstairs by myself, especially at night.

My bedroom was upstairs in the big house and since we didn't have lights, we carried an oil lamp, which dimly lit the way. Alone at night, taking the oil lamp, I would go into my room, climb into my bed, and cover my head. There, I could feel the presence of my mother.

I had chores and responsibilities at an early age. After everyone ate, I had to clean up after meals. I felt like Cinderella, whose stepmother made her do all the work. Yet there was never a prince to come to my rescue. There was nobody there for me. I was lonesome, lonely, alone.

My father did not have any control over anything anymore. He just went along with whatever was going on. He was only concerned with pleasing his new wife. My mother was gone, I was a motherless child, and even though my father was in the house, he was not there for me as I thought he should be.

Speaking about the plantation, we had all kinds of animals. Chickens, goats, horses, mules, cows, dogs, and cats. All the animals had to be cared for and fed. I was young, but I was expected to help with the farm animals and so I worked. Mornings were busy and winters were cold. We rose early in the morning to gather wood to put inside the tin heater to heat the house. We heated water, poured the water into a metal tub, and washed ourselves.

The start of the day included going out to the barn to take care of the livestock. We raised animals and grew all our own food. I had to feed chickens, gather eggs, milk cows. There was a bucket beneath the cows utters to collect the milk. Once the cows were milked, I brought the milk into the house and placed it in an ice box. It was a box with a block of ice inside to keep things cool. Ice was bought from a man who sold three- to four-foot-high blocks of ice for 25 to 50 cents per block.

The blocks of ice lasted about one week if you didn't open the icebox often. We had a wooden stove, which meant we had to collect wood from the outside, put it inside the stove, and make a fire to do our cooking. We got water from a well to cook, bathe, wash clothes, and clean the house.

As a sharecropper, my dad was a tenant farmer. Tenant farmers were supposed to be given part of the crop for rent to oversee the plantation for the owners of the farm. There was cotton, soybeans, peanuts, corn, white and sweet potatoes, cucumbers, strawberries, and all types of melons. The only things we bought from the store was sugar, flour, and spices. On a plantation, parcels of land were distributed in blocks and in our family, it was the older children who cultivated, planted, harvested, and managed the crops.

However, at the end of the year when crops were harvested and went to market, most of the proceeds were all taken from the overseers (my dad in this case) by the plantation owner. It wasn't unusual for farmers to have worked all year and receive nothing because they couldn't read or write because the only time they went to school is when it rained. Rain stopped them from working in the fields on those days.

However, missing so many days from school caused the older children to fall behind. It seemed useless to go if they couldn't keep up, so they just stopped going. Since they didn't know how to keep track of what portion belonged to them and the plantation owners knew it, they took advantage.

I believe being alone contributed to my having a great imagination. In fact, I remember the Sears and Roebuck catalogs that came in the mail. I didn't have the toys I saw in the catalog, so I would cut out pictures of dolls and other toys and make believe I had them. I took bricks and built them into the size and shape of a cooking stove. I used jar tops and placed them on top of my makeshift stove as burners. I used rocks for jacks.

I remember only having one doll. She was large and made from heavy plastic. I loved her so much. One day, I came home from school and found my doll in the pig's pen. Everything I loved or wanted; Ms. P threw out. It felt like I was always in her way.

Not only did Ms. P throw out all my things, but she also got rid of everything belonging to my mother. Gone, removed, thrown away, like filthy trash. The only thing she kept was the new clothes washer my dad bought. However, I wasn't allowed to use that to wash mine and my brother's clothes. Ms. P. washed her and my dad's clothes in the new washer. I had to wash my brother's and my clothes by hand. Washing his clothes was hard.

We hand-washed clothes by drawing water from a well, using a washboard and tub. My brother's clothes were extremely heavy because he wore denim overalls with bibs. Once the clothes were washed, I was supposed to lift the weight of these wet denim clothes, wring them out by hand, and attach them with clothes pins to a clothesline. They were so heavy. Remember, I was eight years old. So, the best I could do is fling them onto the nearby fence so they could dry.

Ms. P's youngest son, John, was the same age as my brother James. One day, James was picking peanuts up off the ground that were left over after harvest. John decided he would take the peanuts from James, but my brother would not let him. Since John couldn't take the peanuts away from James, he got angry, took out a knife, and viciously stabbed my brother. I stood by horrified. Bleeding and wounded, my brother decided to leave home and head to New York. He was 16 years old, going to a place he had never been, and now he too was alone.

When my brother left, I cried. I was more alone now than ever. My mom was gone. My dad was there but always gone with

Ms. P., and now my one and only protector and friend, my brother James, was gone.

I lived with my dad and Ms. P. until I was nine years old, one year and a couple of months after my mother died. I went to the well one day to draw water. Once I had drawn the water from the well, Ms. P's son came along and tried to take the dipper from me so he could have the first drink.

I wouldn't let the dipper go and when I wouldn't let him have a drink, he slapped me. My father saw it, and I don't remember what he said but he immediately got in touch with my sister Betty and sent me to live with her. She told me that my mom had previously told her to be sure to care for me, even though my dad married Ms. P. to take care of me.

I went to stay with Betty in North Carolina until I was twelve years old. While I was gone, Ms. P's son who had slapped me left home. That's when my father came to get me from my sister's house and bring me home to be with him.

My being alone and feeling lonely carried me into adulthood but in a different way. As an adult, I am an introvert, still somewhat shy, and do not like being in front. I prefer to listen and observe more than talk.

I was not taught so many things as a child that growing into adulthood made me afraid to speak up or out for fear that I wouldn't say or do the right thing. Being alone as a child caused me to not like crowds of people. Since I was always played by myself as a child, I still like being by myself, and I'm not really a fan of being bothered by other people.

To this day, I don't like people hugging me and I believe it's because I didn't get hugs as a child, but I do enjoy giving hugs to people I love, especially my children and grandchildren.

I Once Was Lost, but Now I'm Found
By Agnes Holmes

"Every morning, we get a chance to be different. A chance to change. A chance to be better. Your past is your past. Leave it there. Get on with the future part, honey." — Nicole Williams

I wrote a letter to my brother asking him to come get me. He lived in New York and came to pick me up from Virginia. I got a job as a live-in housekeeper in a small Jewish community called Monsey, approximately 45 minutes northwest of New York City. Although it was not my ideal job, it was the only position I could secure because of my limited education, and it provided me with a place to live. The job required me to clean their house and take care of the employers' children. I hated that job.

Shortly after I came to Monsey, my sister Carrie relocated to a small town about 5 minutes away called Spring Valley. I stayed in touch with my sister, so I found out she and her entire family moved near where I was working. Since she was so close, I started visiting her new home.

I really didn't like the live-in working conditions, so I quit and moved in with my sister and her seven children. It was crowded and challenging, but it was a place to live. I always loved being with my family and although the house was packed with people, I felt a sense of belonging again.

Carrie had a friend who worked at a quilt-making factory. While he was visiting, he mentioned that the factory was hiring. I thought, "I need to find another place to work and make some money to support myself." Here was an opportunity for me to be employed anywhere besides working in someone else's home cleaning and taking care of their children. The same family friend brought me an application. I gladly filled it out and took it to the quilt factory. When I got to the factory, I immediately got an interview, and they hired me on the spot.

I worked at the quilt factory for a year until it moved to another state. Since I didn't want to move to the new location, I was unemployed again. So, I searched for another job.

My sister had four daughters. The oldest daughter was Mary. Mary was one year older than me. One day, this tall, dark, well-dressed handsome man with pearly white teeth and white shoes to match showed up at my sister's house. His name was Leroy. Leroy liked Mary but Mary didn't like Leroy.

The next time he came to the house, a guy with him was driving a two-toned red and white car. I love red and this was a pretty car. The car belonged to Perry, the guy that came with Leroy. I didn't know Perry at the time. They visited for a short time and left. Two weeks passed, and Leroy came looking for Mary again, but Mary wasn't home. She was out at a nightclub.

So, Leroy asked me to go with him to find Mary. I said no. He begged me to go with him and I still said no. Then I thought about it — since he knew the guy with the red and white car, I would tell him to go get Perry and come back in ten minutes, and then I would take him to where Mary was. Since I thought Perry lived in New Jersey, an hour away, there would be no way Leroy could be back in 10 minutes. This was my way of getting out of taking him to see Mary.

Ten minutes later, here comes both Leroy and the guy with the red and white car, Perry. Imagine the look on my face when I opened the door and the two of them were standing there. Well, that plan didn't work. I found out later that Perry only lived up the street, literally two minutes away. A promise is a promise, so we all went to the club where Mary was.

One week later, Perry called my sister's house and asked to speak to me. Shortly after, we started seeing each other regularly. Within a year, we were married.

Still unemployed, I used my husband's car to look for work. He never wanted me to work, but I wanted to work so I could be more independent. After all, I had been independent since I was a child. I eventually found a job at Rockland County Infirmary. The infirmary was like a senior's assisted living and hospital combined. I discovered a passion for nursing and caring for patients. I worked there for seven years and enjoyed caring for the elderly.

After Perry and I got married, I also started attending the church where he was a member. I was already attending First Baptist Church in Spring Valley but moved my membership to attend St. Paul's A.M.E. Zion church with my husband. I started becoming more active in the church and meeting new people.

I met a lady named Vannie Gill, who would become my best friend and the godmother to my children. Vannie taught me many things, including how to take care of myself as a woman and my children. Since my mother died when I was young, my stepmother didn't teach me much about becoming a woman. I watched Vannie and learned a lot. Many women in the church influenced me because I was shy and wanted to know so much, I just watched them and emulated what they did. I have to say I've learned more by listening and watching than by talking. It's a practice I continue today.

While working at the infirmary, I discovered I didn't like seeing people die. A new supervisor came, and I requested a vacation. The staff complained that I was going to be on vacation at Christmas time. Before this request, I worked through all the holidays because they were short of help, and I filled in for other aides. This Christmas was the first time I requested off for an entire month.

My husband was taking me and our first-born child to Georgia to meet his family. The superintendent told the supervisor to grant my request because I was always there. The supervisor said in a nasty tone, "I'll grant it this year, but don't expect it next year." That was enough for me to quit even after seven years of faithful employment.

What I liked was watching people grow as I watched my children grow. For two years, I took care of other children as well as my children in my home.

One day, Vannie came to me about an opportunity to work with children in a more structured environment. At the time, she saw a need for children to be cared for in our community but knew she wanted the people serving the children to have the proper education. Vannie believed in education. She set up a meeting with Dr. Romney, who created programs in Early Childhood Development for West Street Day Care Center. The center where Vannie, my best friend, was the Executive Director.

She encouraged me to complete my education so I could work at the day care center. I went back to school, finished my high school education at the local community college, and armed with just the outline of the program Dr. Romney created, finished my associate degree in early childhood development.

Mary Jane, another friend of mine, was the Executive Director at Nyack Head Start, which had a position available. She offered me a position as a head start teacher and under the direction of Carol Dowdy, I received my teaching credentials. Carole Dowdy, the education coordinator, was a stickler for training and sent staff to solidify our skills working with children. Carole also taught me many things about children, life, and myself. She has been instrumental in my development as a person and she and I are still good friends today.

When I look back over my life, I realized these were the obstacles I faced:

- I grew up without my biological mother.
- I felt alone and lonely for most of my childhood.

- I felt abandoned by my father. Though he was physically present, he was emotionally absent.
- Yet, here's how I overcame the obstacles.
- I learned more about God and believed that although my biological mother was not physically with me, God and her spirit guided me.
- I met the people I needed to watch and emulate.
- I was blessed to be surrounded by people who encouraged me throughout my life.

If you relate or find yourself in a place where you feel discouraged, look at your surroundings. Who are you hanging around with? Whom are you listening to? Are the people you're with pulling you up or pulling you down?

The one word that describes the message of my life is "observer." Every step I've taken since I was a little girl was about observing what others did. Most of what I've learned was the result of watching people I admired.

Many people guided me on this journey. However, most of the people I admire also love God and I'm grateful for all my spiritual sisters and brothers that showed me love along the way, including:

- The Little Zoar family in Boykins, Virginia
- The First Baptist Church family in Spring Valley, New York
- The St. Paul's AME Zion family in Spring Valley, New York
- The New Berean Baptist Church family in Portsmouth, Virginia
- The Canaan Baptist Church family in Hampton, Virginia

Thank you for your love and prayers.

Biography: Queen Angles Holmes

Queen Agnes Holmes is an 84-year-old mother of five children, grandmother of eleven, and great-grandmother of twelve. She enjoys spending time with her family, crocheting, cooking, traveling, and keeping up with world news.

She's a mentor who loves God and people. Many people feel her warmth and kindness and call her Mama Holmes.

Her favorite scriptures include Psalm 23, Psalm 91, Psalm 103, Psalm 121, and Proverbs 3:5-6. Her favorite songs are "I Know the Lord Will Make a Way" and "Amazing Grace."

She has an associate degree in early childhood education and spent many years supporting her husband's business, Suffern Auto Radiator, in Suffern, New York.

She's tech-savvy, using her smartphone to send text messages, gifs, and pictures. She enjoys shopping, banking, and working on her computer with Google and YouTube.

She is a member of Canaan Baptist Church, in Hampton, Virginia, and is an active part of the culinary ministry feeding the hungry once per week.

Throughout her life, Agnes has found guidance and support from her church community, which has helped her in all aspects of her life, including child-rearing, marriage, work, and education.

Agnes is a remarkable woman who has overcome numerous challenges in her life to become a beacon of hope and inspiration for others. Born the youngest of seventeen siblings, she learned the value of family and togetherness at an early age.

Growing up in a rural farming community, her parents did not have a formal education, but they exhibited intelligence and love toward their children. However, the pressures of living in racial times and unequal employment opportunities made survival extremely difficult for the entire family.

At the age of seven, tragedy struck when Agnes's mother passed away, leaving her father and stepmother to care for her. For two years, she lived with her father and stepmother until she moved to North Carolina to live with her elder sister, Betty. Despite facing many challenges, Agnes remained close to her siblings and found solace in their family's love and support.

Agnes began her career as a domestic worker after moving to Rockland County, New York, but eventually found her way to working in a quilt factory and then a nursing home. It was during this period that she married Perry Holmes, Jr., and started her own family. Agnes discovered her passion for caring for others while raising her own children and began caring for children in her home. She took great joy in watching them grow and develop.

In 1967, Agnes became involved with West Street Day Care Center, volunteering her services and enrolling her twin boys as students. She found that she loved working with children and continued to do so for many years.

After taking an 18-year break from education, she made the decision to continue her studies in 1974. Despite being a mother with a job, she persisted and achieved her high school diploma and AAS Degree in Early Childhood Education from Rockland Community College, Suffern, New York, in 1981. Throughout this period, she was a salaried employee at West Street Day Care Center and remained there until 1981. Additionally, in 1981, she was offered a better position at Nyack Head Start, Nyack, New York, where she spent the next 7 years. She obtained her Child Development Associate Credential from the Council for Early Childhood during this period.

She's a giver and a supporter of the Natasha House, a transitional home for homeless women and their children.

Agnes loves her family and is the youngest and last living sibling of 17 children. She and her husband Perry Holmes, Jr. (deceased) have five children, Barbara H. Smith, Donna A. Graves, Sheila P. Rogers, and twin sons Perry III, and Terry Holmes. She is a grandmother, a great-grandmother, and an aunt to a host of nieces and nephews who affectionately call her auntie.

Queen Agnes can be reached by email at sisterholmes1@gmail.com.

The Revelation Hurt

By Barbara H. Smith

"There can be no keener revelation of a society's soul than the way in which it treats its children." — Nelson Mandela

At three years old, I was different. A diamond in the rough, as my mother tells the story. One day, while grocery shopping, she saw this adorable teddy bear sitting atop a bicycle. After paying for her groceries, she decided, *I'll buy this toy for my daughter.*

The bear not only sat on top of the bicycle, but it had cymbals attached to its paws, and the pedals were attached to its feet. While the pedals went round and round, the hands and cymbals clapped together. *Fascinating*, she thought. She purchased the toy and left the store.

She arrived home with a bag of groceries in one hand, me (2 ½ years old) and the toy holding onto her other hand. As she took me into the apartment, she sat me in the middle of the kitchen floor to keep an eye on me and thought the toy would keep me occupied as she began to prepare dinner. And it did for a short time. She watched me as I watched the bear, clapping its hands and moving its legs round and round on the bicycle.

But, unbeknownst to her, I took the toy and went into another room. The next thing noticed was I wasn't in the same room. How many of you know that when a 2-year-old is out of sight and in another room, you need to go check?

As she rounded the corner, in sheer horror and disbelief, she saw me sitting in the middle of the room with this toy that she thought was so adorable, and that she had spent her last bit of money on, totally obliterated, in pieces all over the floor.

She was in shock, teary-eyed, and *thinking my dainty little girl is destructive. What in the world?* She turned for what she thought was a moment thinking, *I've got to get the broom and clean up this mess.*

While she was looking for the broom, she heard a different noise that sounded like forks clanking together coming from the same room. How many know when you hear noises, and a 2-year-old is in another room, you need to go check?

This time when she rounded the corner, to her amazement, the toy was completely put back together and functioning, proving that before I was 3 years old, I was an engineer.

Fast forward, I never liked dolls (my mother didn't know that at the time), and I always loved machines and still do, and because of it, I spent an illustrious career in information technology as an engineer. Why do I tell that story? The engineer was always in me, like a diamond buried. Now that I have made the discovery of who I am, I can show up authentically. That's how audacity shows up. I was two and a half years old. *How does it work?*

Don't show me anything cool without showing me how it works. From the time I can remember, I always loved learning how things work. As a little girl, I never really cared for traditional little girl toys. I had little to no interest in dolls or playhouses. Even tea parties and tea sets bored me. I loved tinker toys, Lincoln logs, Lego building blocks, and cars. Even today, I still love cars. I can name every car logo on the market today and when they come out with new ones, I am enamored with those, too.

My ambition for the newest and latest became an obstacle. You see, I'm the eldest of five, and because I existed three years before my next sibling came along, I was always curious and independent. I had my own things. The only one to have my own room and my own toys – the others were not allowed to play with them. I thought differently.

But I always wanted more. I wanted to be wealthy and have all the things I thought I deserved. When I became a mother, I wanted more to leave an inheritance to my children. The *wanting more* drove me to work harder and longer at the expense of spending time with my children. It had never occurred to me that I was neglecting them emotionally. I was driven. It was for them that I worked so hard.

It was well past time that the damage I caused would be evident. In 2020, my father left us. At the height of the coronavirus pandemic, we had to make the excruciatingly hard decision of putting him in a nursing facility. Putting him in that horrible place was difficult enough, but with the virus eliminating the ability to check on him daily, it was horrific.

The last time we saw him breathing was his birthday. The chaplain and nurses propped him up in his wheelchair and did a Zoom session so we could see him. He was unaware of his surroundings. His body was limp, and he was unresponsive when they called his name. They didn't care for him like they would have when we were able to visit. There was no doubt his care was relatively nonexistent when we couldn't see inside the confines of those walls.

On May 1, 2020, in the early morning hours, the phone rang. It was the call that no one wants to get about their loved ones. "Hello," I said. Groggy and trying to see the clock with sleepy eyes, the voice on the other end announced herself as someone from the facility. Her next statement caused me to become enraged. "Your father has taken a turn for the worst," she said. Screaming, I demanded, "WHAT THE HELL DOES THAT MEAN"? She softly said, "He passed away."

There was a silence that seemed eternal. I sat up on the side of the bed thinking, *how do I tell my mother that the man she's loved for 60 years is gone? What will I say to my siblings?* So many thoughts raced through my mind, I didn't have time to think about grief.

Three years have passed since that time, and my sister Donna made plans to spend time with our mother. It was going to be a glorious time for her. She said to me, "I'm going to give you a break." That's a good thing, right? Wrong! Our mother lives with us – me and my husband, Robert, but we have so much fun that I don't need a break from her.

I cherish all the moments we spend together. We have breakfast almost every day together. She shares my stories of triumph and loss in business. She sometimes reminds me of meetings. I didn't really need a break from her, I'm attached to her in so many ways. Well, the day came for Mama to visit with my sister.

It was the first time I'd really sat still for more than just a few minutes. My husband, Robert, was at work and my mother was an hour and a half away from home. I walked past the room where Mama sleeps and started crying. Real tears, big, bold, torrential rain tears. I sat in sobs of grief and realized I was grieving them both. *What is this?* I wondered.

Suddenly, like a massive hurricane ripping through a city and tearing up everything in its path, my heart was ripped to shreds. It was my fault. The problems my children were having boiled down to me. The one who didn't support them emotionally. Their lives were unbalanced for decades.

I was so busy making a living, I neglected to make a life for them. I missed being in their lives and now may be missing being in the lives of their children. *What have I done*? I questioned, I wondered, I pondered the devastation. Is this horrific error causing a legacy of parental absence?

The revelation came so late in life, I was devastated. I cried literally for two straight weeks while my mother visited with my sister. The realization of my father's death and how he died alone brought me to my own absence. Now I, too, have the possibility of dying alone without the nearness of my children.

It was difficult to live with this realization because it reminded me of scripture, "What profits a man who gains the whole world and loses his soul?" I felt like I sold my soul at the expense of my children.

I've been married before and my husband abandoned me. Yet, nothing could compare to the hurt of realizing I had caused abandonment issues for the very ones I loved. My children. I inflicted the pain; conviction is difficult but necessary to come to the surface of the pain especially when you're the one who caused it. I keep thinking *I must fix this*.

But how? That's when I learned about the stages of forgiveness. I must ask my children for forgiveness. I must listen to what they have to say. I must allow them to be angry. I'm still walking through the process. It took years for me to recognize what I did.

So, let me ask you a question. Are you walking around oblivious to the pain you may have caused? Are you willing to pull back the band-aid and reveal the scab that may be affecting generations to come? If we don't stop and take responsibility for causing others horrific pain, the ripple effect has the potential to be far and wide.

Even more painful to note was that the signs were there, but I was so driven and focused on success I was completely blinded by what I thought was the reward. One of the many signs was that my sons ran away from home. Each one of them ran away at different times. They were crying out for help, and I just ignored the glaring signs.

25

When I look back, my father did the very same thing, and his father before him. It was my mother was the one who always attended our sporting events, parent-teacher meetings, and all our school activities. My dad never came. I can't remember him ever attending anything I ever did, and I did a lot. I was very active in school. I looked for his validation around every nook and cranny and never got it. I have since learned that validation is for parking, not people.

I vowed I would never be that way with my own children and the very thing I said I would never do was exactly what I did. Never say never — it's unconscious wounding.

I didn't lean on anyone during this time. In this moment of discovery, I didn't see emotional abandonment as a problem. It was only recently that I even realized what I'd done.

Then, I had the opportunity to be alone with my thoughts and felt alone in the revelation that I was unfamiliar with my children. I didn't really know them. I didn't know what they liked or didn't like. I didn't know their favorite things.

They had been crying out for my attention for years and I didn't see it or hear it. How could I be so blind? Blinded by success. Blinded by the money. I thought, what a horrible mother you are. My self-talk as a coach was, *you can help people around the world but can't help your own children.* The revelation hurt and the two words that describe how it felt... SOUL SHATTERING.

Unlock the Door – My Journey to Forgiveness
By Barbara H. Smith

"To forgive is to set a prisoner free and discover that the prisoner was you!" Lewis B. Smedes

I came to realize that I was responsible for being emotionally absent from my children's lives. I created a void and caused damage. Acknowledging and accepting that I caused something so painful and harmful for such a long time was a monumental step, but it was also terrifying.

I love what Joan Sel said about asking for forgiveness in the South Bend Tribune. I've used these five steps in my forgiveness journey with my sons and taught others these principles in my coaching practice.

Step 1: Recognize.

The first step is to recognize that you have done something wrong. This can be difficult, especially if you are not used to admitting your mistakes. But it is important to be honest with yourself and with the person you have wronged.

The thought of them not being able to forgive me or choosing not to forgive me crossed my mind. The neglect spanned many years, leaving a deep scar. It wasn't until after my father's passing and my mother's absence (she was visiting my sister for two weeks) that I confronted the pain head-on.

27

The experience plunged me into a severe depression for several weeks. I wasn't just feeling down; I was also lethargic, lost my appetite, and developed a skin rash on my arms and hands. The sickness had manifested itself in my skin. To make matters worse, I didn't even realize that I was depressed.

Step 2: Explain why.

Once you have recognized that you have done something wrong, you need to explain why you did it. This is not the time to make excuses. Instead, you need to be honest about your motivations.

In my situation, I was driven by ambition and believed that I was creating a better life for myself and my children. However, the reality was that I craved the attention that came with success: the praise, the awards, and the recognition. Now I realize that I didn't need external validation to feel fulfilled. I had to discover how to love myself more than I believed others loved me.

Step 3: Apologize and ask for forgiveness.

The next step is to apologize to the person you have wronged. This is not easy, but it is important to show that you are sorry for what you have done.

I have individually approached each of my children to ask for their forgiveness for my emotional absence and the harm I caused them. While I had previously apologized for missing some important events in their lives, it was only through writing this that I fully grasped the depth of their feelings of abandonment and the magnitude of their hurt.

Sincere and genuine repentance is the only way to heal such wounds. Through my prayers, hope, and conversations with them, I aim to make them aware that they too must be cautious to not follow in my footsteps and repeat the cycle with their own children.

It is worth noting that my father and his father before him also deserted their children, highlighting the importance of breaking this pattern for the benefit of future generations.

Step 4: Allow the other person to be angry.

When someone is hurt, they have the right to feel angry and express their emotions. It is important to allow them to share their thoughts without interruption and to be empathetic toward their need to be heard. Rather than judging their hurt or comments, it is crucial to actively listen and validate their feelings.

Step 5: Forgive yourself.

The final step is to forgive yourself. This is often the most difficult step, but it is important to remember that everyone makes mistakes. You cannot change the past, but you can learn from it and move on.

Out of all the steps, this one is the most challenging for me. The sadness I feel is so profound that it has made me contemplate not wanting to live. The devastation is lodged deep in the pit of my stomach and in the depths of my heart. Even as I write this, tears of regret, pain, hurt, and sorrow continue to stream down my face.

Despite the pain and sorrow that I have experienced, the story continues, and it is not over yet. As I write this, I am grateful to share that each of my sons has personally expressed their understanding of how my absence came to be. They have forgiven me and expressed their joy in having this time together.

My heart is in the process of healing, and I pray that theirs is as well. I would do anything for my children, and now, when they reach out to me or I call them, I am fully present and engaged now.

I am committed to advocating for parents and young adults that being present is the most valuable gift that they can offer their children. As I have learned from personal experience, the saying, "It's not what you leave for your children, but what you leave in your children that counts" holds true. Therefore, I will continue to encourage and emphasize the importance of being emotionally present for our children.

If you are reading these words, I urge you not to let another day pass without expressing love to those you are connected to by family ties. It's never too late until it's too late.

This is my second anthology project as a visionary author, but the first time I have fully engaged in the writing process. It was an incredibly emotional experience for me, and it clarified why this work is so crucial for all the authors involved. It allowed me to gain insight into the secret places of the heart that need healing.

Undertaking this project requires a deep dive into one's soul. It can be illuminating, but it is not for the faint of heart or those who are afraid to confront their emotions.

In the previous anthology project, *Empowering You: It's Your Time*, I was an onlooker, an observer of the transformative power of the process for the authors involved. However, this time as a participant in the writing, I saw firsthand the evidence of the profound impact it can have on healing past wounds.

Through this experience, I can now attest to the importance of guiding others through this journey toward healing. Putting my painful experiences on paper has left an indelible mark on my heart, soul, and life, and I am certain it will empower others who choose to embark on this journey.

The one word that best encapsulates this experience for me is WISDOM. My previous understanding of wisdom was totally self-centered. I was wise in my own eyes, a smart aleck even. However, through this process, I have gained a deeper, more godly wisdom.

As James 3:17 states, "Wisdom that comes from heaven is, first of all, pure; then peace-loving, considerate, submissive, full of mercy and good fruit, impartial and sincere."

I followed these steps in my journey to forgiveness with my sons. It was not easy, but it was worth it. I am grateful for their forgiveness, and I am committed to being a better mother to them.

I am also committed to helping others who are struggling with forgiveness. I believe that everyone deserves to be forgiven, and I want to help people find the healing that they need.

If you are struggling with forgiveness, I encourage you to reach out for help. There are many resources available to you, and you do not have to go through this alone.

Forgiveness is a journey, not a destination. It takes time, effort, and commitment. But it is a journey that is worth taking. Forgiveness is a gift and can bring healing and peace to your life. I encourage you to reach out for help. that you can give yourself and those you love.

Today, my children have extended their forgiveness to me, and we have wholeheartedly embraced each other with love and gratitude. I am deeply thankful for God's forgiveness and for the chance to receive forgiveness from my sons while we are all still alive and well. It feels as if the prison door of my heart has been unlocked, even though my journey toward self-forgiveness is ongoing, I am filled with hope and faith that healing is possible.

God continues to surprise and amaze. Thank you, God, again for unlocking the door of my heart and making me free, for whom the son sets free is free indeed.

Biography: Barbara H. Smith

Barbara H. Smith, known as the "Celebrity Speaker Trainer," is an Amazon bestselling author, award-winning international speaker, executive coach, and trainer. She is an actor, corporate business strategist, and tv show host.

Her winning edge originated at the intersection of both pursuing undergraduate and master's degrees in computer information technology and her life experience as a Black woman in a white-male-dominated industry. With THIS as her foundation, she founded BHS & Associates, LLC in 2016 and offered customized corporate training programs and workforce development along with personal executive coaching.

Her awards include Astell Collins, Global Inspiration Award, Kavod Foundation, International Service Award, Dr. Greg K. Dillon, Excellence in Action Award, and an appointment as a World Civility Ambassador from the iChange Nations signed by His Royal Highness Sir Clyde Rivers and presented by Special Envoy, Dr. Ruben West.

A media darling, Barbara has made appearances on a variety of tv and radio shows, both nationally and internationally, including The Doctors, Authority Magazine, and more.

Additionally, Barbara is the host of The Empowering You Show, airing live each week on Amazon Fire and Roku.

In all her work and media appearances, Barbara H. Smith uses her time, energy, and platform to help people communicate better by building their confidence with straightforward, easy to understand techniques. Her client list includes CapitalOne, Canon, ALCOA, and Blue Cross/Blue Shield to name a few.

She has a giver's heart and serves the women and children of Natasha House, a transitional home for homeless women and their children. Barbara loves God and her family. She is the mother of three sons, and a grandmother of nine. She currently resides in Hampton Roads, Virginia, with the two of loves of her life, her husband Robert and her 84-year-old mother (mom-manager), Queen Agnes.

To connect with Barbara, visit http://linktr.ee/bhsmith

Hold on Beyond the Break

By Dr. Lillie Grant-Epps

Did you ever feel like God abandoned you and left you with nothing but pain? Well, I have. In 2006, my identical twin sister died. I still remember that morning – even now.

I got a phone call from my sister, Darlene, who said, "Sister, I have to tell you something." I said, "Not now, I'm in a meeting, I'll call you later!" but she kept insisting, "Sister, Nita is dead!!" I dropped the phone and slumped to the floor. My head was spinning and felt as if my Spirit left me.

A coworker offered to drive me to the hospital, and I just sat there thinking, t*his cannot be happening! God would not do this to me.* You see, my God knew everything about me, and He knew that I could not bear this. Plus, Jesus loves me, and He would never take the one person that was dearest to me.

It seemed like hours went by before we reached the hospital – I could not breathe. I went into the room expecting to find that it was all a terrible joke, only to find my Nita lying so still, already cold. I believe that there is power in words so I did what I knew to do – I said, "In the name of Jesus, Nita, rise up, you will not die but live, rise up and live…"

I cannot remember how many times I said those words until I just fell on her body and pressed my body to hers, hoping she would feel me and wake up. You see, we were so close that we could always feel each other. We knew when the other was experiencing a headache; even when we had our children, we felt each other's pains. We were truly knitted together.

I said, "Lord, why? Why would you take the dearest thing to me?" Then I began to bargain with God, "Okay Lord, if you are going to take her, take me too, we came here together in the same womb, we will go out together."

I did not want to leave her. You see, when we were 5 years old, we were sent to live with our Aunt Flossie and Uncle Fire. Aunt Flossie let us know that we were "stray cats" – that no one loved us, not even our own mother, so all that she did for us was "out of the kindness of her heart"!

She was so mean to us and called us names like, "You are Black and ugly – you will never amount to anything! No one will ever love you!" Every day, we heard this.

Me and Nita would look at each other and say, "Aunt Flossie got this wrong" – we loved each other and made a vow to never leave each other and to always take care of each other. I did not realize how powerful vows are until much later. When Nita died, I felt as if I had not fulfilled my vow to her. I didn't protect her, I didn't come to her rescue, I didn't keep her alive and safe... I was so riddled with guilt.

As I prepared to bury my sister, looking back, I don't know how I got through everything. I went out to shop for her last look on this earth, fighting back tears as I picked out the details from a dress, down to her underwear, how her hair was to look, her makeup – knowing that this would be the last earthly memory of her.

Writing the obituary, sharing my thoughts of our love to others at the funeral, riding to the cemetery sitting there as her body was lowered in the ground – I lost it!! How could I put my precious Nita in this cold grave? Especially in Surry County – where we had so many bad memories, never to see her beautiful face again. I failed her! I died with her that day, I was buried with her but moreover, how could God allow me to go through this. I was so angry with God...

Sitting there at the graveside, as they lowered my sister in the grave – I felt my heart stop, I could feel nothing. *Was this a nightmare? Who was I, is this real? Where am I?* I felt numb – *not my Nita, my sister-my love.* How could God allow this to happen? Why?? Maybe God really doesn't love me like He said He did, all the stories of how Jesus loves me... Was it all a lie, or is someone playing a horrible bad joke on me? *I'm dying, I want to die – I can't live without Nita...*

I remember the weekend of Nita's death – she loved bingo, but I hated it. We were mirror images of each other. There was no one I could share my hopes and dreams with but Nita – the only woman I ever kissed on the lips, hugged, and didn't want to let go. We were so identical – we even had childhood scars in the same place. No one could tell us apart. Not even our mother.

With our backs turned, even she would just say, "Nita-Sister, one of y'all come here!" No one could make me laugh like Nita could – usually at the wrong times. I remember sitting with her at a funeral and she started laughing at one of the deacons continually clearing his throat – so funny. She started laughing, then I started laughing, and we had to get up and leave... Of course, they sat us right in front of the church, so funny.

Nita could fight; she was strong. I was afraid to fight – weak. She could talk – I couldn't, so she became the spokesperson for the both of us. I was scared of everything – Nita was bold – I was shy – she was brave and even would beat up boys for me – Nita always had my back – who's going to have my back now? Everybody loved Nita! My mother would say, "Why don't you be more like Nita?"

Losing Nita left such a void. I questioned, "Who am I? Lord, you didn't even let me know that you were going to take her – I always felt her, but not this time." The Lord spoke to me and said, "If I had allowed you to feel what she felt, I would have had to take you home, too. Remember, 'for I know the plans I have for you,' says the Lord. 'They are plans for good and not for disaster, to give you a future and a hope.' Even though you both came here in the same womb, I had a different destiny for you, Lillie..."

I heard a story once about a man who had fallen asleep behind the wheel and woke up in a river. In a panic, he woke up fully convinced that he was about to drown. He felt the ice-cold water beginning to fill the car and he began to cry out, "Lord save me," but the waters kept coming. Finally, as the car continued to sink, the man was able to get out. Now he was standing on the top of the car, but the car continued to sink.

He cried out, "Lord please don't let me die, save me!" The car continued to sink. The man heard someone call out to him, "Catch the rope!!" The man was so relieved. After reaching for the rope several times, he was able to catch it as the car sunk beneath the waters. As he was being pulled to safety, the rope began to break. Again, he cried out, "The rope is breaking, help me – I'm going to die..." The voice cried out and said, "Grab hold of the rope beyond the break..."

The man said, "I can't, I'm afraid to let go, I will surely die." The voice said, "Grab hold beyond the break – I got you." With one big leap, the man grabbed the rope beyond where it was breaking and was pulled to safety.

I love this story because, in life, there are levels of faith – levels of obedience. God will call us to go beyond what seems impossible for us to do – to bear more than we think we can bear. Sometimes in life, our very lifeline begins to break, and imminent death is at hand, but God is able to give us strength to grab hold beyond where our lives are tattered and breaking to pull us to safety. Sometimes, we lose all hope and thoughts of giving up play, in our minds. What's the use? Life is too hard!!

Wanting to Die

I love going to the river. One day, I went down to the river to be alone with my thoughts. It was such a beautiful day with clear, blue skies. I had been to this spot many times before. Usually, I could walk only a short distance on the pier into the river, but I was always hindered by a locked gate that prevented you from going farther.

This day, however, the gate was unlocked; I opened the gate and began walking out into the river. I looked back and saw that I had traveled into the middle of the river, far from shore. Suddenly, the winds began to blow extremely hard, so much so that the waters began to cover the pier. I could hardly keep my balance. Fear came – *how did I get here?*

I heard a voice say, "Go ahead slip into the water – it will be over quickly, you can end it now and you can be with Nita." Tempting – I began to cry as I slipped and fell to my knees with nothing to hold on to. Now water and wind were engulfing me. the thoughts came – *this is it, just let go and let the water take you...*

In the wind, very gently, I heard the Lord say, "I got you – call out to me." I said, "Jesus, save me!" Instantly the winds died down; the water became so still – so gentle. Yes, the winds and waves really do obey!!

Grief can be so dangerous that you lose sight of life itself and become very delusional. I finally made it back to shore safety and cried out to God, thanking Him for saving someone who did not want to be saved. What a Mighty God. ***Jehovah Roi – the God that sees me.***

The obstacles that I faced that almost kept me from my ability to empower others – **FEAR!!** Wanting to die but afraid of dying.

You see, all my life I felt abandoned and rejected, so afraid of everything. Fear of the dark – standing in the hall all night at

Aunt Flossie's house... Nita coming to be with me, standing with me, holding my hand, us vowing to never leave each other. Making up games in the dark, praying for morning to come – so afraid. Hearing Aunt Flossie's voice, "You are nothing – no good, Black, ugly, not worth anything; no one loves you." but I would whisper under my breath, *Jesus loves me!!*

The obstacle of fear warped my ability to trust others and trust myself. It resulted in low self-esteem, including no confidence, poor self-image, and self-hate. I could not trust others or open up to them. I feared that no one would ever love me. These obstacles affected me emotionally, physically, personally, and financially throughout my life.

Emotionally – lowering Nita into the ground – I promised her that I would never leave her. I will always take care of her, remembering how many times she was there for me in the darkness, reassuring me of her love and that I am not alone.

Don't fear, sister – I am here. You are not alone – no matter what you are going through... Yeshua, Messiah - Jesus the Christ will never leave us. Hallelujah.

Personally, I was so self-destructive. I did not have any self-worth, still hearing Aunt Flossie's voice saying, "You are nothing and never will accomplish anything."

That changed the day my name appeared on the bulletin board honoring second graders on the Honor Roll. Everyone congratulated me, saying that they wanted to be just like me.

I made up my mind that day that my name would never come down from the bulletin board – it never did! I learned that I was smart and that I could determine my – Aunt Flossie was wrong!!

Physically, I used food to fill the voids in my life – the abandonment by my mother and father, the rejection. I gained weight and always saw myself as ugly and fat. No one would ever love me, anyway. This was one of the hardest areas to overcome. Even now, it takes determination, discipline, self-control, and hard work.

Every day, I must choose – I must put in the work, if not, I will choose to take comfort in food instead of choosing the guidance of the Holy Spirit. *Faith without works is dead.*

I learned how to love my body by editing the tape that I listened to for so many years – acceptance and taking charge of my life by surrendering to God and finding the true "Comforter." The one who will hold you in the middle of the night, in my darkest hour and whisper, "You are mine; I will never leave you – you are beautiful, fearfully and wonderfully made."

My body suffered from self-destruction and abuse: weight gain, quadruple heart bypass surgery, two heart attacks, respiratory failure, hypertension, diabetes, diverticulosis, and arthritis. My sister died of a massive heart attack – I had two heart attacks and heart surgery – Grace and Mercies.

God said, "I have a different destiny for you Lillie." That destiny has taken me to the White House and to speak on the steps of the United States Supreme Court championing the Cause of Life, leading many to the Lord across the United States and around the world.

"Those who are wise will shine like the brightness of the heavens, and those who lead many to righteousness, like the stars for ever and ever," – Daniel 12:3. Thank God that He had a plan that did not end with the death of my sister.

Finances were horrible. I could not buy a brown paper bag, and no one would loan me one. Over the years, God showed me that if I continue to work for others, they will always determine my wealth. Remember, Aunt Flossie said I would never amount to anything because I had no worth.

God said, "Start your own business and you determine your worth." At age 60, I started Family and Child Empowerment Services (FACES), which is now a multi-million-dollar business, starting my own business afforded me the opportunity to not only be able to acquire generational wealth for me and my family but provide jobs for others to do the same. I just celebrated my 70th birthday, all because God had a Plan.

In this seventh decade of life, I've started Lillieworks, Inc., a 501(c)3 a non-profit organization formed to address and empower women of color to find their purpose by changing the narratives of how they see themselves and find worth. Lillieworks is part of God's plan.

Weeping may endure during the night, during the season of sorrow, but Joy comes in the morning with every provision –

emotionally, personally, physically, and financially – not necessarily in that order. I want to die empty, having done all that God wants me to do to give to all He has called me to give to. I want to hear my God say, "Well done!"

Agreement is the key: God instructed Job to agree with him and the result would be peace.

"Agree with God, and be at peace, thereby good will come to you. Receive instruction from his mouth and lay up his words in your heart. If you return to the Almighty, you will be built up" - Job 22:21 ESV. We often say things that overrule what God has said about things and then we wonder why our prayers are not answered.

Agreeing with God will always bring you Peace and clarity. Once we come to a place of agreeing with God, we understand that He is in Control in ways that our finite minds cannot comprehend. Further that we must make that confessing with our lips that God is in Control – thy will be done.

Words have great power. In fact, the Bible says that the power of life and death is the tongue. Proverbs 18:21. Prolonged grief will cause us to linger in dark places, some self-destructive. Agreement not only brings peace but gives new hope – new direction.

Agreement brings a new level of trusting God and God promises, *"You will keep in perfect peace those whose minds are steadfast, because they trust in you"* Isaiah 26:3 (NIV). Not agreeing with God will cause us torment, living without peace.

The confessions we make and the conversations we have with others are very impactful. By speaking and confessing the positives of God's Word, our words have the potential to add life and promote peace to ourselves as well as others.

Speaking negativity will have the opposite effect; it will cause things to become worse, even unto death. A lot of our troubles begins and continues because we refuse or neglect to humble ourselves before God to inquire of what words to speak and by becoming disciplined in the things we speak and confess."

Grabbing hold beyond the grief will give you renewed strength, new focus, new purpose. It will give you time for healing, time to take a breath, find hope and realize that life is not over despite the loss.

Keep Singing

By Dr. Lillie Grant-Epps

When Nita died, I stopped singing. We had been singing together since age 3. My mother would make us matching outfits and have us sing at church. I hated it, Nita loved it... it made my mother proud.

I became so critical of others – withdrawing from everyone and almost became a hermit. I remembered being invited to a Women's Conference and was told that they would be honoring twelve women in the community, and I was one of the twelve. I attended reluctantly, questioning why would they want to honor me?

As the night went on, they got up to announce the Honorees, myself included. I sat there as they presented big, beautiful Mary Kay baskets loaded with all kinds of gifts and products. I was the last to be honored. I sat there, wondering what I was going to get. The Mistress of Ceremony called my name, Dr. Lillie Grant-Epps. She paused and said, "Oh, I forgot to get you a gift! But here, take this book, I am so sorry." Embarrassment, shame, and rejection consumed me.

Thoughts flooded my mind... they were not Godly thoughts... *Oh no she didn't! She obviously does not know who I am, I have been to the White House, I met with the President of the United States Counsel on race relations, and you forgot to give me a gift?* I rose to the occasion, put on my best smile, and accepted my little book with all the thank you Jesus and so much gratitude – but I was furious.

The other ladies carried their beautiful baskets to their cars, and I took my flimsy book and threw it in the back of my car – mumbling all the way. That book laid in the back of my car so long I forgot that I had it. Until one day, while cleaning out my car, I came upon it buried under trash and clothes. Something said, *pick it up.* I did and read the title: **31 Days of Praise**. Something said, *read it.*

I started reading and this book – this unwanted gift – changed my life. This little book was of much more value than a Mary Kay basket. I could not put it down. It may have had 50 pages in the entire book filled with God's promises, quotes, and praise. Again, I am repenting to God for forgiveness for being so arrogant and entitled.

This was my favorite quote in the book, which still lingers in my spirit:

> *Our griefs cannot mar the melody of our praise; we reckon them to be the bass part of our life's song, 'He hath done great things for us, whereof we are glad.' It is the burning lava of the soul that has a furnace within – a very volcano of grief and sorrow. It is that burning lava of prayer that finds its way to God.* — Charles Spurgeon

I decided to sing even if all my notes are bass notes, and even through times of pain and uncertainty. You see, bass notes anchor the melody... they hold everything together. They bridge the gap, providing a rhythmic and harmonic function at the same time. I have found my song – a song of Praise and Thanksgiving… no longer bound by guilt, shame, and fear.

I had to go to Colorado Springs shortly after my sister died. I really didn't want to go. I felt like I had nothing to give. A good friend of mine, who had also lost her identical twin sister, convinced me that I needed to go and encouraged me to expect God to speak to me and bring me healing. I was in Colorado for a week and didn't hear a thing from God. On the last day, I was rushing to the airport down the mountain when I was blinded by the sun – so bright I had to pull over. I couldn't see. It was then that God spoke.

> *"Because he has set his love upon Me, therefore I will deliver him;*
> *I will set him on high, because he has known My name.*
> *He shall call upon Me, and I will answer him;*
> *I will be with him in trouble;*
> *I will deliver him and honor him.*
> *With long life I will satisfy him,*
> *And show him My salvation."* Psalms 91:14–16, NKJV

God's ways are not our ways, nor His thoughts our thoughts. I began to cry and asked God's forgiveness for being angry with His taking Nita. I realized that God gave her to me for a season and she was His to take. He knows best. Thank you, God, I will trust you, Lord. Help me to fulfill your plan for my life.

Grief – the experience of coping with loss. Most of us think of grief as happening in the painful period following the death of a loved one. But grief can accompany any event that disrupts or challenges our sense of normalcy or ourselves. This includes the loss of connections.

There are five stages of grief:

1. Denial (I don't believe they are really gone)
2. Anger (I'm so angry that they are gone)
3. Bargaining (I promise I'll change if they come back)
4. Depression (I feel hopeless about my future without them)
5. Acceptance (I can go on with my life and deal with their absence)

Most people who experience a death go through these stages. Not everyone experiences them in the same order, and some people stay in one stage longer than others. For example, one person may be in denial about a death for a few days but stay angry for several months. Another person may only feel angry for a week but feel depressed for much longer.

It's especially important to remember that everyone experiences grief differently. There is no specific way to feel grief. Let's say one of your friends dies in a car accident. You may experience it much "harder" than your other friends, or you may seem unaffected while everyone around you is struggling to get through it.

After you acknowledge that you are grieving, what do you do about it?

Four ways to ease grief:

1. Talk to someone about how you feel. Bottling things up will only make you feel depressed and alone. Many people have experienced the same types of feelings that you have and will understand.
2. Write a letter to the person that you lost. When you're done, either stash it away or rip it up. It feels good to talk to the person (even if it's on paper).
3. Share great memories of that person with friends or family members. Plan a meal or gathering where you can each share your favorite memory of that person and how they made your life better.
4. Make a memory box or book. You can include pictures, stories, or other things that remind you of that person. Pull it out when you want to think about them and connect with your feelings. When you are done, put the book or box away to pull out again at another time.

It's okay to feel sad and hurt. Don't try to stuff, hide, or ignore your feelings. If you get so sad that it begins to affect your daily life, it's time to ask someone for help.

Hectic schedules can drain your energy and keep you so busy that you often forget to take care of yourself both physically and emotionally. Take a moment to stop and think about what you need to do to enable you to perform at your absolute best. Regular self-care can improve your well-being and self-esteem. It also increases resiliency that you need to help you to bounce back when problems come up in your life.

So, what does self-care look like, and what can you do?

Nine steps to taking care of yourself:

1. Tell yourself that you do matter; and because you matter it is important to spend time and energy on helping yourself feel better. Self-care is finding a way to build yourself up.
2. Be extra nice to yourself. Do things that you enjoy and that help you to relax and unwind.
3. Be patient with yourself. Accept that you will make mistakes, know that you can't please everyone, and allow time to grieve. Know that things will get better, even though it might take a while.
4. Invest in yourself. Follow your dreams. Study things that interest you. Establish a faith walk for yourself.
5. Recognize when you are in problems over your head. Sometimes, this means that you need to admit that you need someone to throw you a safety line; this could include working with a therapist, talking to a trusted friend, or going to a support group.
6. Say no to situations or people that you know could trigger you in a negative way. Self-care means that you protect yourself so you can build a stronger future self.
7. Think about things that happened in the past and learn from them, so you don't repeat the same pattern. Self-care means taking time to really evaluate if situations and relationships are healthy and if they should continue.

8. Focus forward. Self-care means moving ahead, not looking back. Making goals for tomorrow or next week is your first step toward the future.
9. Be proud of yourself. Declare victory when things go well. Recognize when you make good choices, or when you succeed at something that you have been working toward.

The next time you hear "take care of yourself," remember these nine points. They can be effective in your life, and result in a stronger YOU!

Grief isn't one size fits all. One of the most important things to understand about grief is that there's no specific way to grieve, and everyone grieves differently. This can also be one of the most confusing things about the grieving process.

Typically, you aren't the only one experiencing a loss. For example, the death of a family member means that the rest of your family is grieving as well. The challenge comes when you realize that everyone's grief looks different. Sometimes, conflicts with friends and family members can happen because everyone grieves differently. This conflict can be frustrating and even make you feel isolated in the way that you are grieving.

What can you do to cope with that?

- Remember that there isn't a right or wrong way to feel when grieving.
- Take time for yourself, but don't isolate yourself.
- Spend time with other friends and family to give yourself space from those who are grieving.

- Respect other people's grieving processes like you want them to respect yours.
- Find healthy ways to express your feelings.
- Take care of yourself physically. Grieving is demanding work!

Questions to ask yourself: Are you?

1. Stuck? – make a commitment to let go.
2. Still grieving your loss? – Help is on the way.
3. Angry with God and life? Anger is a healthy emotion – God said to be angry, but do not sin. However, if you hold on to anger too long, it will destroy you. Anger, unresolved, will turn to bitterness and consume everything in its path, including you.

- Don't be a victim – don't allow yourself to be consumed with grief that you lose you!
- Agree with God it will go well with you (Job 22:21).
- Design a plan of self-care.
- Seek help – you are not alone.
- Live…

Find out God's plan for your life and be determined to be faithful to fulfill your destiny – His plan. Jesus is the Prince of Peace – He has given us the Great Comforter. Did you know that God's answer to every conflict, every hardship, every distress is Peace?

Peace comes from agreeing with God's decisions. "Agreement with God affords us the opportunity to ask anything and be assured that we shall receive the petition of our lips by our Father in Heaven," Matthew 18:19.

Death can come in many ways. Some people just check out of life – choosing drugs and alcohol addiction, some abandon their families and themselves. They become "walking ghosts on the earth," strung out and overwhelmed by demons of addiction and self-defeat. Don't allow yourself to be killed by demonic spirits. God has given us His Spirit – Life-Giving, Life-Affirming, and Life-Overcoming. Don't let your Spirit die in your season of grief. Agree with God!

I once facilitated a drug support group for co-dependency. Here is Lolita's story:

Lolita's husband was addicted to drugs and alcohol. There were times that her husband would come to the meetings with her but even when he didn't come, Lolita came alone. I remember she shared that she had bought her four children Christmas gifts and her husband, who had totally abandoned the family by then, broke into the house. He stole the pictures off the walls and all the kids' gifts to go out and buy crack.

One night, I asked Lolita how she was doing. She said, "I'm fine – Did you hear? I moved!" I wondered what she meant, so I asked her. I knew her circumstances – that she was left alone to raise her children alone, her husband arrested for drug distribution. I thought to myself, how could moving change things in her seemingly hopeless situation?

She replied, "I moved under the shadow of the Almighty and I have Peace. I agreed with God regarding my husband and my life. I realized that there was nothing I could do but trust my God, who promised to supply all my needs. I got on God's page and stop insisting on my own way."

"He who dwells in the secret place of the Most High shall abide under the shadow of the Almighty. I will say of the Lord, 'He is my refuge and my fortress; my God, in Him I will trust.'" – Psalm 91:1-2 NKJV.

Conclusion:

There are few people who will ever deal with the loss of a twin. Any loss, however, is still a loss, and loss results in grief. It could be the loss of a spouse, parent, child, sibling... any relationship including the loss of a pet, divorce, loss of a business, finances, loss of self, etc. Loss is loss.

Letting go, trusting God, accepting the process of recovery is the only answer. For there is a time and a season for everything under the heavens. A time of grief is part of those seasons. Embrace your season and give yourself grace – extend kindness to yourself.

Death and loss are something we will never understand. One day there is life, you feel their breath on your skin, you hear their voice, you kiss their lips, you feel their touch, you remember the laughter and even the tears, you remember making promises and sharing secrets. It's okay to remember and to hold on to all of that. It's even okay to cry. Everyone grieves differently, and there is no set time limit for grief to end.

Remember, God says that He is Alpha and Omega – Beginning and End and as a result He is outside of time and space – Life and Death. Hold onto God's promises to you – knowing He is in control. He is Yahweh. Yahweh means *"He brings into existence whatever exists,"* 1 Samuel. At the right time

– the right season, your grief will have run its course. I am confident that I will see my sister's face again in Glory forever and ever. Amen – Until then, I will keep on Singing...

Dedicated to the memory of Faye Anita Grant, my twin.

April 21, 1953 – February 7, 2006

Biography: Dr. Lillie Grant-Epps

Dr. Lillie Grant-Epps is a qualified mental health professional (QMPH) for families, adults, and children. She has had years of first-hand experience in the field of mental health counseling, including pastoral counseling and marriage and family therapy.

Dr. Epps has seen a lot in her lifetime, and she realizes that compassionate care goes a long way. She understands that it's not always how much you know, but how well you demonstrate how much you care. She is committed to always taking a role in providing solutions rather than contributing to society's problems – being an integral part of our community by assisting individuals with mental health struggles to become stronger. Strong individuals make strong communities.

Dr. Lillie Grant-Epps has been a licensed and ordained minister since 1999. She is a recipient of a Bachelor of Science in Human Services Counseling from Old Dominion University, Master of Divinity with a concentration in Women's Ministry, and Doctor of Ministry in Theology from Providence Bible College & Theological Seminary.

Dr. Epps is the founder and owner of Family & Child Empowerment Services, Inc. (FACES), founded in 2009. FACES was born out of a desire to provide quality community-based mental health services with dignity and compassionate care. The goal of FACES is to empower individuals and families, equipping them with tools for a lifetime, promoting success and independence.

One of her favorite quotes is by Anthony J. D'Angelo... "Without a sense of caring, there can be no sense of community." FACES is committed to becoming that caring, cutting-edge agency.

Now Dr. Epps aspires to utilize her years of experience in developing a Non-Profit organization, Lillieworks. The word combines lilies and work (Lily-works). A lily is a floral ornament that has a Biblical reference to signify that "The work is complete." Dr. Epps believes that Lillieworks is her swan-song ministry, completing her work. The overall goal of Lillieworks is to see lives changed and transformed.

Dr. Lillie Grant-Epps can be reached at: (757) 921-4407

3717 Willow Glenn Circle

Suffolk, VA 23435

Email: lgepps71@gmail.com

Website: www.facesinc.biz or www.lillieworks71.org

Lost Without Hope: The Obstacle

By Donna A. Graves

"We are soldiers of the cross, we've been found to reach the lost." — Randy Travis

My story starts long before the trauma that took my "want to" away. I was molested at the age of 16 by my paternal uncle. This young and impressionable child was groomed and didn't even know it until that day.

That day, I lost my innocence and found mistrust in all males. I was incredulous that one of the "cool" people in my life at the time would take something that wasn't theirs and did it with blatant disregard for me.

I trusted this person with information that made me a target. I had insecurities about being Black in a predominantly white school. The middle girl of five siblings, I thought my parents had their hands full and I was confident that I could navigate the world with minimal assistance from the grownups.

Always curious, I was in the 11th grade of high school and wanted to take my bicycle on a ride to get my legs ready for track practice. I was in my workout shorts and green and white warmup jacket. The first stop was to the corner store for some snacks and then to my favorite uncle's apartment for some sweets before heading to practice. I was riding up the main road in our suburban town and waved at people I knew along the way. It was a warm spring day, and I stopped at the light to take my jacket off.

By the time I got to his apartment, I saw my younger sister was already there and put my bike down next to hers. As I climbed the steep steps to his place, I was singing some song I had heard on the radio. I was quite pleased with what I had planned for the day and, for that matter, the rest of my life.

In the minutes prior to this life-changing event, I was on top of the world. It was spring, I had gotten really good grades, and it was about to be summer. What else could be better? I knocked on the door and my sister let me in. I greeted my uncle with a hug as usual.

Something wasn't right. I don't know how I knew, but it felt different. There was another man in the apartment at the table. Someone I didn't know. My uncle introduced him as a "friend," and I spoke... because I was trained to speak. He was creepy.

I went to the fridge as normal and grabbed a soda. Sat down at the table across from the man and he asked me how my day was going. I responded, "Fine."

My sister was sitting at the table as well, eating some cookies. I felt sick and when she asked me if I wanted one, I said no and told her we should go. She was not interested and just sat there. Several minutes passed, and we all just sat around the table while my uncle continued to stand near the stove.

Then, he went to his bedroom. Around 5 minutes later, he called me and said he had something he wanted to show me. I got up from the table, glad to be away from the creepy man, but I didn't want to leave my sister with him.

I was thinking that I would go see what my uncle wanted and then make my sister come with me by saying I had gotten my period or something that would be urgent, and we would have to leave immediately. When I got to the door of my uncle's room, I took one more look down the hall at my sister, who was still eating cookies.

When I got in his room, he was on the bed, and the TV was playing some pornographic movie. I had seen Playboy magazines before and knew what naked bodies looked like. I wasn't impressed. What happened next, I was not prepared for. He asked me to sit on the bed, and I said I didn't want to. I was still standing, and he grabbed my hand and pulled me down on the bed.

He started to take my shorts off before I could get up off the bed. He was over 6 feet tall and at least 180 pounds. I was 5' 6" and about 110 pounds. The next thing I knew, he had put his hands in my panties, and I just kept saying "WHY are you doing this?" This is not right.

I started to scream, and he put his hand over my mouth. He said to me, "It is better for me to do it than anyone else." I froze as I couldn't believe what was happening. He tried to force himself inside me and finally, I guess because my body wasn't responding, he gave up and got off top of me. He told me that if I told anyone that he would say I was lying. I was crying, grabbed my shorts, and ran out of the room and down the stairs.

My sister was still sitting at the table eating cookies. She came running down after me and asked me why I was crying and what was wrong. I was so ashamed that I had let myself be taken advantage of. I was angry and wanted to puke.

I told my sister we were leaving, and for one of the few times in our lives, she listened and did it without a fuss. We got on our bikes and rode home. I couldn't sleep or eat for days. I started having nightmares when I was finally able to sleep, so it wasn't for long. I cried all the time.

I couldn't and wouldn't tell my parents. I made my sister promise she wouldn't, either. She was worse than a bad refrigerator, she couldn't keep anything! I started to act out — talking back, smoking, drinking. Whenever my uncle would come to visit us, I would not be anywhere alone with him. I would sass him, and my mom and dad would yell at me and tell me to apologize. I wouldn't and would leave the house instead. I hated him. I wanted to hurt him like he had hurt me.

Months went by and I didn't see him. I was in my final year of high school and did the best academically. I was ranked in the top quarter of my class and was crowned Homecoming Queen, "Ms. Afro," (a local service/social beauty pageant) and received honorable mention and an acting scholarship from the New York Academy of Theatrical Arts from the "Ms. Empire State" pageant.

Politically, I was senior class president and president of the New York Conference, Long Island District youth council for my church. Athletically, I was on the track team and captain of the varsity cheer squad. I had roles in school plays and musicals, was in the band, in the choir at school and church, and played piano. Again, I was on top of the world, I received a full scholarship to my first-pick school and had offers from several others. All was going well.

Then, trouble started my first day of college. I was talking smack all the way from our house to the campus. How I was glad to be leaving and was not going to miss anyone. My mother and Godmother drove me to school. It was exactly 30 minutes after we arrived that my mother said, "Well, okay, see you soon. Love you." I couldn't believe she was just going to drop my stuff off and leave me there... with strangers!!!

Oh, you know I made a scene. Then, as if on cue, God sent an angel in the form of a young woman named Shannon Mallory. She told my mom I would be alright and that she would take care of me. I was a wreck. Tears and snot all over the place. Shannon took my bag and showed me to my room on campus. We were down the hall from one another. As I finally calmed down, we went to get something to eat. We went back to the dorms and talked for several hours.

That day was another that changed my life. Shannon became my best friend. The next day, God sent me another angel. She really was an angel, an Alpha Angel — she was a sweetheart of the fraternity. Her name is Carmela and we three became the "three-amigas" on campus. We didn't do everything together, but we always knew where each other was. I found a new family.

Navigating college, especially that first year, is tough. As I began to settle in, there were men all around, and lots of them! They looked great, no they were FINE! I had a few boyfriends in high school, but it wasn't like this. I started to like them! What was going on? I guess I was too busy before to really notice or have interest. The few that I did find attractive were either not interested in me or already had a girlfriend.

I started to get that same queasy feeling that I felt with my uncle. I didn't know what to do. So, I would cover up and not wear tight or revealing clothes. I didn't want to draw attention to myself. I was told one time that even if I put a potato sack on, I couldn't hide what was me.

The casualties of the molestation were a loss of identity, intimacy, and curiosity. The loss of freedom to express myself. I found promiscuity and self-loathing. I was depressed as I was usually the only Black person and woman in most of my classes and/or social events.

I was pursuing a degree in the sciences, and the white males let me know on more than one occasion that I was not wanted, nor in their opinion could I do the work. I even found exclusion, isolation, and ostracization from the people that I looked like and had community with. I got called names like "Oreo" or "white girl." I also got asked why was I trying to be white? This was because I found myself to be the "smart" one. I was really only trying to live. I wanted out. Out of my town, out of my school, out of my family, out of this world.

At the end of that first year, I had to take a class over in summer school or risk being put on academic probation. I lost my scholarship and had to get several jobs to make up the difference. At the university, I had a racist honors English instructor, and she failed me and the only other Black person in my class.

After that, my ability and confidence to write was impacted as well. This impostor syndrome also affected my ability in the rest of my schooling. What did I do wrong? Why didn't I get it right? I was a good girl, I did what I was told, I followed the rules, and still I got mistreated.

I face this obstacle every day. Each time I am ignored, each time my voice is silenced, every time I get questioned or question my own self-worth and intelligence, I am traumatized all over again. A feeling of victimization, being subjected to "otherness" by white people, white women especially, is exhausting.

I can go back as far as elementary school. On several occasions, I was taken out of the class a placed in the hall at a small desk because I was "acting out."

The incident went like this. The class was doing reading and math skills. The teacher (a white woman) asked a question. No one raised their hand to respond. I raised my hand and gave the correct answer. She asked another question to which no one responded.

I raised my hand again and she said *let someone else answer*. I waited several minutes and again raised my hand, to which she completely ignored me. So, I yelled out the answer. In response, she pulled me out of my chair and took a desk and put me outside the classroom. I sat there until the period was over or it was time for us to go to lunch. This happened several times.

Eventually, my sister's 4th grade teacher (another white woman) came and got me to do my work while her class was at lunch. I spent many hours in the principal's office. Boredom will do that.

My mother tells the story that I was a problem child in lower grades because the school would constantly call and say, "Donna won't do this, or Donna is doing that." "Donna won't eat, or Donna won't talk." I finally said to my mom one day, "I can't be wrong all the time, and they can't be right all the time. Sometimes they lie!" I still got my butt whipped.

One time I even made the principal mad. We were headed to assembly, and he came down the hall and told us not to lean against the wall. I guess I didn't move fast enough, and he yelled at me, and I told him he made me sick. He said, "Get her out of my school!" and immediately suspended me for the rest of the day. I had to have my parents come pick me up. That wasn't a very good day.

Still another time in the summer, me and my sisters were going to the town pool near where my dad had his auto shop. My mom would drop us off at the pool and we would stay there and swim for most of the day while mom took my brothers with her and would work with dad.

We would get our lunches packed the day before. They included a soda that was wrapped in aluminum foil and put in the freezer and either bologna and cheese or a peanut butter and jelly sandwich, with potato chips and cookies or a piece of cake. We had our cooler bag and would sit in the hot sun as there were no shade trees. We were ashy and crispy.

After we waited for the required time for our food to digest, we would also wait to hear the whistle signaling that the "adult swim" was over, and we could go get in the pool. As soon as we would get in the pool, all the white people would get out. I thought it odd at first, but then I was like, we get the whole pool to ourselves!! Eventually, they figured out that we were not going anywhere, so they would get back in.

In middle and high school, which we got bussed to, I was usually the only Black child in my classes, and I was ignored most of the time. I began to lose confidence in my ability to accomplish anything. Still, I would do my best.

When you are constantly told that you are dumb or stupid and you are no good at math or science and only useful for making babies and cleaning the house, you start to believe that lie and others like that about yourself.

Well-meaning comments about how cute I looked or any comments about my shape sent me to a dark place. That is the shape that got me into trouble in the first place. Loss of self-confidence and being dismissed occurred over and over.

Another time, I tried out for the school musical, and I was the only Black person period in the lineup for the roles. I tried out for the lead in this musical and after auditions the next day, the call back list was posted. My name was at the top of the list!

I was so excited and when I came in the following afternoon to challenge for the part, my name had been moved to understudy, and the lead was given to a white girl in my class who couldn't carry a tune in an empty bucket. This role had a scene in it that would have me kissing a white boy. I declined the part as understudy and worked with the music director as an assistant.

As I write these recollections, my anger, disappointment, and sadness again emerge because these hurts have been buried for such a long time. It is like a drowning person gasping for air; you only have enough energy to take the next breath before you go under for the last time.

I began to use negative and defeating self-talk. How could a God that I love and worship allow things so horrible happen to me? I began to question my faith and try to figure out if this is what happens when you are crossing all the "t's" and dotting the "i's." If so, then what's the point? I lost my joy. I felt abandoned by God, my parents, and my family. This was multiple layers of devastation.

Opportunities and goals that I would have attempted I didn't even investigate because my self-talk said I wasn't good enough, so why even try? More recently, I was working for a government contractor and was asked by my manager to provide innovative information for a project. I worked up a proposal and presented my ideas at an executive level meeting.

I felt quite pleased with myself and the team that I had assembled. After that meeting, I was told that the same manager (a white woman) was going to be replaced with another white woman. This new manager had been demoted previously for being a micromanager and disrespecting her employees, and now she was given the team that I was working on because it had high visibility.

I continued to work with my team, and within the first month after the new manager was there, she started to dismantle my team and required me to train what I now know was my replacement, a white male. As I did my best to explain what processes I had designed and implemented, he was unable to catch on and get it. He told the manager that I was uncooperative and was not giving him what he needed to move the project forward. I got called to the director's office and was demanded to teach this man, to respect my manager, and to "behave" myself.

I went home every day with a headache. I began to impute these horrible thoughts to my children and spouse. I became overly sensitive to anything that they would say. I was angry all the time and knew why but didn't know how to fix it. My family, whom I love, was walking on eggshells. I eventually went to seek help from a counselor.

I was constantly anxious. Any loud sounds would make me jumpy. I had a terrible time sleeping and so there was constant fatigue, and my resilience was not what it used to be. I used to be the "Energizer©" bunny! At that time, my body was showing signs of stress — I was having autoimmune breakouts, my joints hurt at one point to where I couldn't lift my arm, and after many trips to the doctor, they said I had a bone spur. But before that, they basically said it was all in my head.

Without the confidence and ferocity I once had, I could not and would not pursue opportunities that could improve my family's financial situation. I felt broken and defeated. My spouse and I began to argue about money and why we couldn't figure it out. Instead of me being affirming and supportive to my spouse for the opportunities he was working, I derided his efforts and sabotaged his ego.

Worst yet, my children were watching their mother crash and burn. It produced in me an inability to trust people and intimacy became difficult. I did not want to be vulnerable, ever. I know that there are systemic problems, especially in the U.S., and the rules are not the same for everyone.

Being subjected to microaggressions daily is exhausting. Not knowing who you can trust is also a huge burden. Again, all the well-meaning folks without action to support the words suggest that there are no issues. But there are issues. Because you don't see them or choose to acknowledge them, they are still here and real.

All sorts of experiences may cause similar feelings. For example, people who may be dealing with or are living alternative lifestyles and they do not have their family's acceptance or support. I have several relatives of different orientations, and they will usually not show up to family events because of how they or their significant other are treated.

Shunning is a real thing, and it doesn't just happen with religious sects. Families that have children of different parentage (mixed race) experience shunning, and the one that most Black people don't talk about is colorism. If you "got" good hair and green or grey eyes, some families will celebrate you. Most will look at you and ask, "Where did you come from?"

Any situation where trust has been broken and the person must navigate life in a world that is constantly changing can be problematic. You may have worked for a company for many years and there is a change in management. Suddenly, you have a layoff, pink slip, or text of termination, or you are being asked to take a severance package. It could be that a security guard comes to your desk and tells you to collect your personal belongings and escorts you out. Now what?

People who are having mental incapacity and feelings of being stuck within their minds and there seems to be no way out for a winning outcome and they want to choose death over life. Finding out a diagnosis that is terminal and you must tell your family.

71

Originally through this period, I had very destructive behaviors. I became a work-a-holic, drank too much, and smoked cigarettes. To calibrate my behavior, I eventually began taking long walks on the beach and praying for insight. I began reading the Bible and motivational materials more. I began journaling, which I used to do before.

Writing prayers, affirmations, and goals that I wanted to accomplish gave me focus. I had several great friends and family that helped by praying and walking alongside me. The main thing that helped me was getting into a rhythm with my life listening to music, singing, playing piano, and listening to my body.

I am still healing, even though I am blessed and heavenly favored. We each go through situations, but you go through and come out on the other side transformed.

Reclaimed: Brand-New Life

By Donna A. Graves

"Although no one can go back and make a brand-new start, anyone can start from now and make a brand-new ending." —Carl Bard

In the midst of my soul's sorrow, the seeds were planted of how to survive, and to sustain success. The steps unearthed surpassed my expectations as they began to sprout. Now I will share the fruits of that labor.

1. Become Aware.

Take stock of where you are and how you are. How are you responding to stimuli? Do you feel grounded or anxious? Self-reflection and journaling are key to becoming aware. At this point, you may have the feeling that you can rise above air. It's fine... you can!

This awareness can be affirmed by enlisting the aid of a trusted observer, proposing the proceeding questions, and carefully listening to the responses.

2. Acknowledge and Assess.

What is it that you need to calibrate? If you are not where you wish to be what should you change? Admit; own; confess and be honest with yourself, name what you have found helpful, be kind about what may not be pretty, and allow yourself some space to process. Journal.

3. Take Action.

Allow for forgiveness, and that includes yourself as well as others. Begin to pray for healing and well-being. Get help, professional or otherwise, if necessary. Journal.

4. Celebrate Transformation.

Do something to honor the change in you. My favorite is to get lunch and go to the beach, put my feet in the water, and thank God for walking this journey with me. Journal.

I purposely seek opportunities to use my life to empower the lives of others through my gifts of hospitality and encouragement and they have served me well. With each opportunity that is presented, I ask the question, "How is God leading me in this situation to show more love? Where is there a need that I can help fulfill?"

I pray with and for those who have needs that I cannot assist in my current situation. I continue to investigate innovative ways to make this world a better place.

The message the world should receive from me is that my super Empower is providing small acts of kindness that lead to great feats of love for myself and others.

The word that I believe describes my life's message is *mindfulness*.

Mind your own business. I have heard it said that when you invest 50% of your time on minding your own business and

50% on leaving others' business alone, you do not have any time left to meddle in another's affairs.

It takes the same amount of energy to be about your own life as it does to armchair quarterback someone else's life or provide unsolicited input. Could it be we are too afraid, too envious, or lazy to put in the work?

Mind what you say and to who you say it. We spend most of our waking hours talking to ourselves. What are we telling ourselves?

If it's not healing, hopeful, and heavenly minded, be quiet and listen to the truth from God's instruction book, or other inspirational material. We have one mouth and two ears for a reason. Listen more and you'll be surprised by what you hear.

Mind your p's and q's and your manners. Be kind, hospitable, mindful of etiquette, and pay attention to the details. There is an adage in sewing and woodworking: *"Measure twice and cut once."*

In the carpentry trade, it literally means 'one should double-check one's measurements for accuracy before cutting a piece of wood.' Otherwise, it may be necessary to cut again, wasting time and material. In essence, though, it means to plan and prepare thoroughly and carefully before acting.

Mind your dollars and cents. "A fool and their money are soon parted" — Dr. John Bridges.

When I was young, I was told to obtain and maintain a good credit score, save my money, and should I have extra (yeah right) to invest. Then "adulting" happened, and all things free went the way of the dinosaurs.

Sadness ensued and the dreaded budget word became an unwelcome companion until the debt was reduced, bills were getting paid on time, and I didn't fear the phone ringing. Imagine that!? Freedom from fear. Developing a plan for where my income was going was so totally radical that the first time we were able to have a completely cash Christmas, I cried.

Mind your health. If you are not physically, emotionally, or spiritually healthy, it becomes difficult to manage life much less live abundantly. You could gain all the money, but good health is priceless.

Additionally, a way to expound on mindfulness is to assess my life in terms of how a mining prospector from the past would. They went in search of treasure and adventure.

Mine for gold. What knowledge or wisdom have you acquired? There are acres of diamonds in your own backyard. Better yet, pick up a book, listen to a podcast, take an online class.

Your altitude is directly proportional to your attitude about acquiring new information. The information should provide you with tools to assist you to enjoy this life.

Mine for hope. Look for good in all situations. Through all adversity, pain, discouragement, and grief I have maintained hope.

Without hope and the power of the Holy Spirit, there would be no me. In the most challenging, even life-threatening situations, I have maintained my sense of hope.

Mine for the future — not only yours, but for others. Be of service to others. There is a current saying of "Pay it forward." Jesus paid it all, so we can at least pick up the tip.

Whenever the opportunity arises, and it is within your capacity, lend a hand. Volunteer, provide service via a meal or ride to the store. In order to gain life, you have to give it away through your time, talent, and energy.

Finally, when I was young, I participated in high school and college as a track and field athlete, I never won a race I didn't start. Meaning keep at it.

My life isn't perfect and sometimes it isn't pretty. Persistence, and perseverance have helped me prevail. The more you practice living empowered and empowering the lives of others the easier it becomes.

Biography: Donna A. Graves

Mrs. Donna Amanda Graves has been a disciple of Jesus Christ since 1969. In 2001, Donna and her family became members of Carver Memorial Presbyterian Church, Newport News, Virginia.

She became an ordained elder in 2013 and serves many ministries at the local and presbytery levels. She has served as the Presbytery of Eastern Virginia's (PEVA) representative on the Synod of the Mid-Atlantic's Permanent Judicial Committee (SPJC) and Convenor of PEVA pilgrimage community.

Married for 34 years to Nathaniel Graves II (deceased 2019), they have two adult children: Nathaniel III and Raymond. They have two grandchildren, McKenzie and Nathaniel Anthony IV.

Donna retired as a process improvement project manager in the engineering department after 18 years of service. As the lead for the sheet metal Value Stream at Huntington Ingalls Industries, Newport News Shipbuilding, Donna and her team implemented many cost-saving projects.

Mrs. Graves is well educated, currently in her second year at Union Presbyterian Seminary pursuing dual degree programs, Master of Divinity, and Masters in Christian Education. She holds a master's in engineering management from George Washington University and a Bachelor of Science Degree in Biology from State University of New York (SUNY) college at Brockport.

Donna has received many awards and certificates including a Certificate of Lean Practice from Old Dominion University, a Certificate in Client Server Management from San Diego State University, and she was awarded Black Enterprise Magazine's Black Engineer of the Year 2012.

Donna is a Toastmaster International Distinguished Communicator and Leader. She is also a member of Zeta Phi Beta Sorority Inc., an entrepreneur, and winner of the Daughters' of the American Revolution citizenship award.

You can contact Donna via email – naxc.mom@gmail.com.

Words Are Powerful: Self Discovery
By Marcia Stewart

"No weapon formed against me shall PROPSER; it won't work." — Fred Hammond

Aggressive, loud, angry, and rough around the edges. Have you heard these words used to describe your behavior? Do you feel these words were intended to make you feel less than who you are or to be made to feel invisible? Were these words attributed to why your progression in career or personal endeavors stagnated?

If these words or any of their synonyms have been used to describe your behavior at any time in your life, take this journey with me to discover how to move beyond the **words.** How to move beyond the setbacks caused by the emotional, physical, financial, personal, or professional stress triggered by the impact of words.

Growing up, the saying "sticks and stones may break my bones, but words will never hurt me" was used as a way for youths not to let "words" defeat them or break their spirit. As a child, I said this many times, and it wasn't until writing this chapter that I thought about the fallacy of the phrase.

As an adult, we know sticks and stones may break bones; however, we know that bones will heal. On the other hand, once uttered, words will hurt emotionally, cause self-doubt, cause behavior to manifest that is perceived negatively or differently than intended, and will remain in the subconscious far longer than it took to speak it.

This chapter focuses on the impact words have in a professional environment and how the use of words can cause behaviors to contribute to the stagnation of one's career. That's right, words you've heard or been told about yourself can manifest in a way that causes **YOU** to limit your professional growth subconsciously.

Think about the terms aggressive, loud, angry, and rough around the edges. What are your initial thoughts? Have you heard these concerning how your behavior was perceived at one time or another? Continue reading to learn more about how I allowed these words to manifest in behavior that limited my professional growth.

Aggressive

The word **aggressive** had been associated with my behavior when I was passionate about a topic, excluded when I should have been included, and persistent when being ignored.

I did not see myself as belligerent, hostile, violent, or out of control at the time. Yet, this is the perception others had of my behavior. An example of my behavior being seen as aggressive was when I was in a collaborative session with peers from other parts of the organization.

The expectation was for everyone to provide ideas to effect change based on the subject at hand. As ideas were presented, everyone chimed in with their thoughts on the validity of the ideas to bring about the desired change. When it was my turn to present an idea, it was received with little discussion and comment.

As the discussions progressed and ideas were presented, a peer presented my idea verbatim, but this time, it was received as a viable idea. Once the ideas were discussed and additional comments were asked for before moving on, I commented about how the idea they just raved over was exactly what I presented earlier.

When I questioned why it wasn't a viable idea when it came from me, I was met with denials and comments that they "didn't realize" that was what I said or meant. After denials of the obvious dismissal of my idea and that it was not intentional, the meeting continued.

I didn't foresee that my questioning labeled my behavior as aggressive. Being labeled as aggressive during meetings caused others to change their behavior toward me by inadvertently leaving my name off meeting invites (meetings I was supposed to attend), not recommending me for projects I had the skill set for, and intentionally overlooking my input and ideas when I was not in the room or conversation.

Instead of my question making others realize their unintentional biases manifested in the dismissal of my idea and made me feel invisible, they saw me as hostile and out of control.

Loud

Truth be told, I am **LOUD**, really, I am. When I whisper, I am loud. Being loud, for many, is natural; they have always been loud and will always be loud. That's me, I will always be loud.

However, I have learned to lower my voice so it doesn't carry. Learning to lower my voice was not my idea; it was not an epiphany that came to me one day. It was a moment when after a meeting, a leader came to me and told me to get on his calendar.

When we had our meeting, our discussion was around me yelling during a meeting (as he is telling me this, I am telling myself, "Yelling? I wasn't yelling!"). My perceived yelling caused the audience to turn off and not hear anything I had to say. As the conversation continued, he explained that I had a naturally loud voice, and since the room we were in was small, it appeared I was yelling instead of talking and holding a conversation.

After the meeting, I began to self-reflect and think about when I was in a group, and people were staring, whispering, or slowly moving away to try and distance themselves from me. Or when I was in meetings, people seemed to be standoffish and didn't leave with the message I thought they should have received.

It was then I realized my being loud displayed a yelling behavior, and it was cause for embarrassment for some. Although I did not realize it then, when others were standoffish or distanced, I was somewhat self-conscious and curious about why they behaved that way.

Angry

When I think of someone being **angry**, I often wonder what happened to them for them to be so angry. My mom always used to tell me that only dogs get angry. As I thought about the word angry, I had to think back to an experience where I was truly angry, not hurt feelings angry, but true anger, and what I felt at the time.

While in the military, I was selected to participate in a two-year program where I could go to school as a full-time student and remain on active-duty status. Being selected was an exciting opportunity, and I needed to prepare myself and my family for the transition. The challenge was that I was on shift work and could not properly plan for the transition. So, as protocol dictated, I requested dispensation and sent it up the chain of command.

As the request moved up the chain, one of the leaders met with me and expressed the concern that my request would not be approved based on the reasoning I provided. The leader recommended I say I had childcare issues.

Now, any military person knows that childcare should NEVER be used as a reason for dispensation. Although this was the recommendation, I clarified that this was not my reasoning and should not be mentioned on my behalf.

Of course, the leader ignored my request and shared the childcare message up the chain of command. So, once it went to the next level for approval, I was not allowed to explain my reasons for the request, I was chastised and raked over the coals for not being responsible enough to take care of my responsibility, a responsibility that I made a conscious effort to undertake, and that was not issued to me when I was issued my seabag. I was upset as I sat there and was not allowed to interject, speak, or deny the false allegations.

At least in my mind, I was just upset. Even when my immediate supervisor came to check on me, I thought I was just very upset. Now that I think back, my supervisor came to check on me because of the looks I gave the leader who lied on my behalf and how angry I was. As I look back, I can say I was angry.

I was angry because I felt powerless and helpless. My anger was expressed with tears. Tears because of the hurt of the betrayal, the feeling of having no power, and the helplessness of being unable to do anything about it. Being placed in a position to show my anger caused my supervisor to look at and treat me differently and watch me closely to be sure I kept my anger in check. And think, I only reacted in anger because I was against a rock and a hard place.

Rough Around the Edges

Having your behavior described as "**rough around the edges**" is insulting because you are being called unrefined. Okay, it makes me think back to when I was a child and got the lecture before leaving the house on knowing how to act in public. Having your behavior described as rough around the edges is akin to not knowing how to act in public.

Although I cannot think of a professional instance when this has happened to me, I wanted to briefly touch on it because it resonates with the words described in this chapter. When behavior is described using aggressive, loud, and angry, the behavior is viewed as unacceptable and should be changed.

Having your behavior referred to as unrefined, uncultured, or unacceptable may cause you to question yourself and your actions. When attributed to your behavior in a professional environment, the words no longer allow you to be judged for your wealth of knowledge, leadership, or the value you offer but for the perceived behavior of words.

Moving Beyond the Words

Remember, words are powerful. They are powerful because once spoken, they cannot be taken back. Once spoken, words like aggressive, loud, angry, and rough around the edges manifest into weapons. Weapons that cause feelings of invisibility, self-consciousness, powerlessness, helplessness, and of unacceptableness. These weapons may have allowed you to behave in ways that have caused "YOU" to limit your professional growth subconsciously.

Continue this journey with me in my next chapter, **MOVING BEYOND THE WORDS**, to learn how to take the behaviors associated with these words (weapons) and use them as weapons of your own. Remember, ***no weapon formed against you shall PROSPER; it won't work.***

Moving Beyond the Words

By Marcia Stewart

"To FAIL is NOT an OPTION, to stumble and fall is a POSSIBILITY, to get back up is a MUST." — Marcia Stewart

Moving beyond words did not happen until I was in my late forties. No one event started me on my journey, and no catalyst spurred me on. There was only a moment.

A moment where I had a lot on my shoulders, so many things coming at me at once. A moment when I remembered *no weapon formed against me shall PROSPER.* A moment when I knew *failure was not an option* and that while I was down, I had to *get back up*.

Through this moment, I decided, "To FAIL was NOT an OPTION, to stumble and fall was a POSSIBILITY, and to get back up was a MUST." I needed a plan, a process, a starting point. Using my knowledge of problem-solving and training development, I began to build a guide that would allow me to move beyond the behavior of the words that held me captive emotionally, physically, financially, personally, and professionally. The portion of my journey I am sharing is self-reflection and how I moved beyond the words aggressive, loud, and angry.

Self-Reflection

First, I took time to self-reflect and find out who I was at that moment. Not who I was five years ago, a year ago, or six months ago, but who I was at that moment. To do that, I had to take inventory of everything that led me to where I was emotionally, physically, financially, personally, and professionally.

This was the moment of truth, the moment when I had to accept myself as I was, the good, the bad, and the ugly. To do this, I made strips of words or phrases that described or represented "the things." Once all things were written, all were placed in piles based on likeness.

At this point, I arranged everything in piles by the different areas in my life that were causing the upheaval in my feelings. For this chapter, I will share the actions I used then and now to conquer the behaviors associated with aggressive, loud, and angry words.

Listen – Digest – Process

If you feel invisible, self-conscious, powerless, helpless, or unacceptable, **DO NOT SAY A WORD**. That's right, keep quiet. I know that when you are in the moment, it's hard, but you must keep quiet.

Keeping quiet looks like the following:

- If you are in a meeting, hold your lips together, doodle on your notepad, and look anywhere except at the offender.

- If you are on the phone or on a conference call, press the mute button and say whatever you want.

- If it was via email, pull up a blank email, do not put a name in the To: or CC: fields, and type away, expressing all of your feelings.

- If you are in a crowd where you can excuse yourself, go to the restroom, to your car, or anywhere you can vent, pace, or cool off.

- If you have someone you can trust, call them and vent.

Doing any of these will prevent you from behaving aggressively, loudly, and angrily. These "keeping quiet" actions allow you to listen to what is being said, take it in without interrupting, digest what is said, and take a moment to cool off. When you finally respond, it will be thought out and delivered gracefully.

Acknowledge the Behavior

After self-reflecting and identifying "the things," I had to acknowledge the good and the bad behaviors. Knowing what causes behavior is easier than acknowledging that you must work on behavior that reflects on you poorly.

Correct the Behavior

The best example of this is my LOUD behavior. If you recall, I admitted being loud and had come to terms with it. Although I came to terms with it, I had to correct the behavior to remove the stigma. There were several actions I took:

- Disclaimer before meetings – When I find myself in a small room, I always start with, "This is a small room, and my voice tends to get loud in small rooms. If I get loud, let me know so I can lower my voice." Once the disclaimer is out, I can normally recognize when I get loud. If you don't want to make a disclaimer, have someone in the room with you that you can trust to signal you when you start to get loud.

- Accountability partners – Let those around you know that you are working using your inside voice when inside and for them to let you know when you are loud.

- Be receptive when being corrected – Once I let everyone know I was working on my inside voice, I had to be receptive to being corrected when I indeed was loud. An example was when my son and I were out to dinner, and he asked me, "Ma, why does the entire restaurant hear our conversation?" My response was, "I'm not using my inside voice?" He said, "No, Ma," and laughed.

Let Go

This last step was the hardest for me; sometimes, I still struggle. Letting go means that once you've identified the behavior, you must leave everything behind that led you to that behavior. Let your trials and tribulations be your lesson, your growth.

Take what happened to you and grow from it. Become the ONE that will NOT allow someone else's actions to cause your behavior to limit your potential. Your ACTIONS are what people see, but your WORDS can discount those actions because of how people hear them.

Move Beyond the Words

YOU MUST ENDURE. Having ENDURANCE means that you made it through the storm. It does not mean you won't stumble along the way. Without endurance, you don't get back up when you stumble and fall. Remember, "To FAIL is NOT an OPTION, to stumble and fall is a POSSIBILITY, to get back up is a MUST."

Biography: Dr. Marcia Stewart

Dr. Marcia Stewart is a retired Navy Veteran who uses her experience and knowledge in workforce development to build and grow the workforce and leaders of tomorrow.

Marcia works with organizations and individuals as a consultant in identifying ways to grow engagement, leaders, and employees, and improve day-to-day operations.

Marcia continuously gives back to the community through her volunteer efforts with Veterans, youths, and the community.

If you want to work through words that hold you back, go to Marcia's website, marciazconsulting.com, to download a worksheet that walks you through the process. If you want to learn more about empowering yourself, sign up for a free 30-minute empowering session.

From Hope to Pain to Gain

By Lucy Wairimu

"The pain you feel today is the strength you feel tomorrow. Pain changes people, but it also makes them stronger." — Stephen Richards

Have you ever experienced pain at a young age and thought that your life and future were ruined? That was me as a naïve teenager – crushed and not knowing what the future holds. Just like any other teen, I had high hopes and dreams for a brighter future. I had just cleared my secondary school education and was waiting to join college.

From my real-life experience, I can bodily testify that however much the pain changes us, you can either come out better or bitter.

I came from a humble background – the third born in a family of seven. My mom ran a small business to boost my father's income. I'm sure you will agree, raising seven children is no joke! Most of the time, it was my mother and me at home in the village with my younger siblings who were still in school.

I was a slim, tall, light-skinned girl with a gap between my front teeth. They say it's a sign of beauty in my African culture. My parents were Christians, and hence I loved church and sang in the local church choir.

I had hopes of becoming someone like my friend, Jane. As fate would have it, that never happened – at least not the way I had envisioned. I remember as a teen, our teacher told us that when we obey our parents and God, we will not fall into temptations. Unfortunately, I had to learn that lesson the hard way.

Jane was a neighbor in my village. She was a couple years older than me and had already finished college. After pursuing a course in accountancy, Jane had found a job in a neighboring town. The town was a two-hour drive from home, and she was commuting daily. I used to admire Jane, and we eventually became friends. In all the neighborhood, Jane was somehow the only young girl I admired. She was neat, good looking, and had a good character to crown it all.

As luck would have it, Jane got a better job offer in Nairobi, the capital city. She would be working as an accountant with one of the government's departments. Early one morning, Jane came knocking at our house. Luckily, I was the one who answered the door. Jane broke the news about her new job, and I was so happy for her – I couldn't wait to one day join college and follow Jane to the big city.

In addition to sharing her good news, Jane also encouraged me to try my luck at her former workplace. She would even introduce me to her former boss and act as a reference. You could see my last tooth as I jumped up with excitement! I knew if I got the job, I could support my siblings and ease my parents' burden a little bit... maybe even save for college.

Now the problem was how to convince my mom that I should pursue a job offer two hours away from home. Well, I took a bold step and ran with excitement to where she was standing. "Mom, something good has come up!" She pulled a chair and asked me to be quick about it – she had lots of morning chores to attend to.

My mom listened attentively to my good news, but she was hesitant to approve until she had discussed it with my dad. The only problem was the job offer was urgent and could not wait until the end of the month when my dad would come home.

She had no option but to agree, but not without wanting to know what kind of job it was. "It's keeping of records," I answered. Not sure what records, but I had to give her something. As a mother, she was concerned about her young daughter commuting daily to a place far away from home – she could only commit me to prayer.

I was happy. My first job was in a town far away from home. It was the beginning of a journey. I had never worked and had no experience. My national ID card, which you receive once you turn 18, was still under processing by then.

It was a Monday morning when we embarked on our trip to Isiolo, a town in the eastern part of Kenya. It was a small town then, and the only landmark was Barclay's Bank. One of the semi-arid areas in Kenya, the town was dusty and the population low.

Jane and I arrived at our destination. It was a crusher, where stones were crushed into ballast. The place had a perimeter wall like that of a prison. There was also an office block and a housing unit for the workers. I could only see men working at this place, no women. The place was very dusty, and the workers there looked funny with dust covering their faces. I guess health and safety was not a worry then, unlike today.

I got the clerical job – my first – with no experience or training to speak of. Guess what? I was also the only woman among 30 men, ranging in age from 20 to 35 with a handful of older men. Phew! Having been raised with boys, I had developed a tough skin and had nothing to worry about. The issue of commuting daily was solved when I was given a single room in the staff quarters.

There I was – a young, beautiful woman manning a quarry, managing 30 grown men, selling ballast, keeping records of sales, banking, and other daily duties. My friend, Jane, instructed me on what was required and trained me for a week before she left. By God's grace, I managed.

I was very hardworking, and my boss was impressed. I still had dreams of going to college, which was still my first priority. I could even take part-time classes, but that was impossible then. Working from Monday to Saturday was already exhausting for me, and the climate was harsh. As fate would have it, my dreams were shattered.

"Eric" (not his real name) was a handsome, tall, dark guy I met on one of my routine trips home on weekends before resuming work on Monday. It was a Monday morning, and I was hurrying to catch a bus to be at my workplace early. He was about 22 then and standing with two other equally good-looking guys. "Hi, excuse me, I am Eric, and these are my friends," he said. "Yes, how can I help you? I'm in a hurry," I replied.

Well, Eric jotted down his number; I jotted down mine, and I took off. There were only landlines in those days, and I was lucky we had one at work. Eric and I started talking, and he was the first man to tell me, "I love you." I was excited and we kicked off our relationship. I was young, he was older, and sometimes when in love you think with your heart and not your head. It felt nice to be in love for the first time. I was head over heels. Eric lived two hours' drive from my workplace, but he would visit.

I forgot all the warnings and advice and discovered I was pregnant. *How could I get pregnant from the first time?* I took several pregnancy tests but couldn't believe I was indeed expecting. What do I tell my mom? What will this guy say? That I was careless?

I blamed myself. Worry, shame, and confusion hit me so badly that I could hardly eat. My colleagues noticed that I was no longer the happy, jolly girl I used to be, but I never told anyone.

Well, at least I knew Eric had a job. Maybe, just maybe, raising a kid would not be an issue... or so I thought. I called him and explained the situation. Later, I shared my fears in a long letter. I learned that Eric was still under probation at his workplace and his pay was not enough for both of us, let alone enough to raise a child.

He, too, had siblings in school and his parents were not well-to-do. But he gave me his word that I should keep the baby and he promised to take care of us. He told me I "shouldn't do something stupid." Eric knew that the hardest part would be telling my mother, and of course I knew that my dad would hear it from her. I could not face her.

Where do I start? She warned me and kept reminding me that we have enough responsibilities, and I should focus on work and saving money for college. Now here I was, one year after getting a job. Pregnant, confused, and fearing the unknown.

My pregnancy wasn't showing. I was round and plump so no one at work knew. When I was eight months along, I had no choice. I woke up very early, packed my clothes, and left the camp. I never resigned – I simply disappeared never to return. I think I was too ashamed and worried that people would judge me since I lived at the camp with only men. Honestly, however, my colleagues loved and protected me, and no one ever messed with me.

My mother was devastated by the news. When I arrived home, she immediately noticed (mothers have extra eyes...). The scolding was unbearable. Her words were laced with anger and bitterness – yes, I was the first girl and daughter. Yes, I let them down.

My father would be home soon – end of the month, he always comes home. I was so scared of what the outcome would be. I never left our compound and would wake up very early in the morning to help around the house. I was very active and would go to cultivate the land before the sun would rise. I would still get harsh words from my older siblings and parents that would tear my heart to pieces.

I used to sit under a tree and cry my heart out. My mom and dad loved me, but the shame I put on them was what they could not stand. Eventually, they accepted the reality of the situation – thank God.

One fateful day, I received a letter through the address of a primary school nearby. The letter was in a big envelope with my name on it. I was excited and then surprised to see that the letter came from the United States – Charlotte Airforce Base.

I didn't know anyone from outside the country, so I was really curious. Turns out the letter was from Eric, who I hadn't heard from for some time.

Eric had received a training opportunity and was out of the country. It dawned on me that I was in this alone. My mom found me reading the letter and an outburst occurred. "He's sending letters? Is he sending *money* for the baby's needs?" That's an African mother for you – now that I am a parent, I understand the frustrations she was going through.

I became depressed. Our home was near a main road so whenever I heard a vehicle stop, I would rush outside to check. In my mind, I could see a vision of Eric coming through the gate. It wasn't easy – though my mother was tough on me, she still displayed that motherly love.

Later on and as time went by, she accepted the situation and embraced me. Dad also softened up, but the labels assigned to me hurt my heart deeply – *she got pregnant, she's a single mom,* and other bad comments cut to my core.

I was 19 when I became a mother. I gave birth to a bouncing baby boy on the morning of November 9. He weighed just 3.4 kg (7.5 pounds). My labor had started suddenly while I was helping on the farm. When my water broke, I thought I had peed myself. I had no labor pains, so I never thought it was time.

When I jokingly told my mother about "peeing myself," as an experienced mother she knew. She took a quick bath, changed, and asked me to do the same. She was about to leave to call for help when my labor pains began. The only neighbor who owned a car was away – the only option was to send someone to flag down a car from the main road. There were no landlines then that we could use to call for help.

"Mothers are angels sent from heaven." I thank God that my mom went to school and knew exactly what to do, but she was so scared that she cried with me. Later, the newborn baby and I were taken to the nearest hospital for a checkup, and both of us were fine.

Eric was miles away. No letters, no communication – we lost touch. I had to swallow my bitter pill and the journey ahead looked gloomy. Here there was a baby to raise – I had no idea how, but I found solace in the word of God. "I will never leave you or forsake you," Deuteronomy 31:18.

I was broken but had to rise above my situation and make a decision. I asked myself, *is this the final nail in the coffin of my dreams? Will I stay in the village like other young girls my age and get married as a second wife to one of the old men in the village?* No. No.

I renewed my relationship with my God, and prayers became part of my life as I struggled to raise my child. I had no job or source of income, but I resorted to helping at the farm to be in good standing with my folks.

Through pain and hardships, you can come out defeated and give up on your dreams or emerge with a new passion. I ignored the warnings – my faith and morals. I got involved in something that I was not supposed to at the time I learned a lesson through my pain and shame. I am now instrumental in helping others, and I do it by leveraging my pain.

"Once beaten, twice shy." Life as a teen mother affected me emotionally, physically, financially, and personally. Living with my already struggling parents and having an additional mouth to feed was a real challenge. It also drained me emotionally, knowing very well that Eric was aware I had his baby.

Eric's lack of support made me sad, and it actually affected my relationship with men. I had trust issues. Though I had a baby, I still looked great, and I would get other young men throwing glances at me. I developed a phobia of men where no amount of "I love you" would convince me otherwise. My focus was only on my child.

Because I was now a mother, my age mates would not socialize with me. I couldn't even go to church for fear of being discriminated against. Being a single mom was a shame in those days. Having to depend on my parents for everything my son and I needed was shameful. The financial crunch was real, and even getting basic items for the baby felt like survival of the fittest.

I had to worry about what to tell my son about his dad when he came of age. What would I say when he comes home from school saying, "Mom, other kids brought their dad to school"? I was feeling really lonely and wondered why a man could sire a baby but not support the mother.

I had to learn to multitask. The workload at home was greater, and I still helped at the farm, which was the source of our food. I do not blame my parents – they eventually embraced me and the baby (forever grateful, Mom and Dad). I may not have realized it then, but were it not for my parents, life could have been much harder. I'm not saying it was a smooth ride, but I was in better hands there than otherwise.

When he was 6 months old, I could leave my baby at home as I ran errands. During market days, I would set out to buy groceries. This is where a lady introduced me to what she was doing to make money. She had a small baby, too.

"I go early in the market, buy beans from the farmers, and by mid-day I can sell the same beans for a profit of 1 shilling per 1 kilogram," she explained. Later at home (remember, I had to be home in time to breastfeed) I got to thinking about what she said.

Trying something similar would affect how much time I could spend with my baby, but I could get a little cash from her business idea. I got a loan from my mom, and when I made a profit, she was happy. I was happy that I was doing something to support my baby.

On the other hand, I was a new mom with health issues to consider, so I could only do so much. We had no house help, and my mother was always at the farm. There was no one to leave my child with. Sometimes, I would wait until he was asleep to rush somewhere.

I was very likely depressed. It's something I know can happen when we give birth in our teen years since we are not ready or prepared psychologically. I knew giving up was not an option. My relationship with God, a positive mindset, and a will to overcome my challenges kept me going.

From my personal experience, life as a teen mom is not just difficult to deal with, it also drains you emotionally and physically. Becoming pregnant as a teen has a host of consequences, like being judged and being limited in what you can become. In addition to the negativity toward you, the child may also suffer from physical, cognitive, and emotional problems – unlike those that are born and raised by both parents in a conducive environment.

As a young mom, going through changes can be traumatic, especially if you do not have a support system. I experienced the stress of being abandoned and stress about how my life would turn out. I had to be very careful about what I did and said in that environment less I get into trouble. This led to low self-esteem and loneliness, as well as feeling like a financial burden.

I had to be very careful about expressing myself. At times, I ended up keeping it bolted inside with no one to share what I was going through. People think that since you had a child at an early age, you'll never amount to anything. It's devastating.

In my case, the most difficult challenge was whether to leave my child with my parents while I looked for a job. They were already financially struggling, so how could I add to the burden? What about the emotional impact it would have on my child? And, really, what kind of job would I get with a high school certificate and no formal training?

Having someone to lean on when you are going through hard times is important. Unfortunately (or fortunately), sometimes all you have is yourself. I had to be strong for me and my child.

I was fortunate that my greatest pillar, comforter, advisor, mentor, and role model was none other than my mom. But above all, I was brought up in a Christian background, seeking God's intervention and knowing there was a Father in heaven who cares for me despite my shortfalls, and he was only a call away.

I rededicated my life to the Word of God and these words reassured me and gave me strength during those low moments. That's who God is – a friend who will never leave you nor forsake you.

"Fear not for I am with you. Be not dismayed, for I am your God. I will strengthen you, I will help you, I will uphold you with my righteous right hand," – Isaiah 41:10.

My mom – I now know better. She was my greatest pillar, comforter, advisor. My midwife – she risked everything and helped me deliver my bundle of joy. Though our relationship was initially strained, eventually she came through for me. My dad (may his soul rest in peace) indirectly supported me financially through my mom, and I will be forever grateful.

Hope in Adversity

By Lucy Wairimu

"Hold fast to dreams, for if dreams die, life is a broken-winged bird that cannot fly." — Langston Hughes

Through my challenges, I was able to balance and work out ways to fend for my kid. My mom stepped in and took over the responsibility of raising him until I was able to take over the responsibility fully. God has been gracious. I gave my son the best education and later fostered a child from an orphanage – something I never thought I would do based on what I had gone through.

This birthed my calling and love for vulnerable children. I later founded a nonprofit organization that provides basic needs to vulnerable children, orphans, and widows in my community. The organization is now celebrating 13 years since its inception. Through my philanthropic engagements, I have received honors both locally and internationally. I am a girl child civility ambassador and a family civility warrior, affiliated to international organizations.

When you feel like hope is gone, look inside yourself, be strong, and you'll finally see the truth – that a hero lies in you. In life, you may have lived long enough to experience drought. However long the drought took, it was eventually broken by rainfall. My story is one that will give you hope and courage to look beyond your adversities. The pain we go through today is a learning process that prepares us to identify our purpose in life.

Holding on to the past can be a conscious decision, just like letting go and moving forward can be a conscious decision. One thing that connects us as human beings is our ability to feel pain. Whether that pain is physical or emotional, we all have experiences of being hurt. What separates us, though, is how we deal with that pain. If we get stuck in thinking about what "should have been," we can become immobilized in painful feelings and memories.

Letting go and letting God gave me hope to look forward to another day. When we believe in God, it makes all the difference because you have someone to look up to. His words of affirmation and promise kept me going. I discovered by letting go that I had to have self-love. Yes, I messed up, but I should not look like the mess I made. I had to dust it off and focus on my future and that of my beloved child.

I looked around. There were people in worse situations, navigating through life challenges the best way they can. It was up to me to wake up and make a decision to love myself and show myself compassion. I had to start being gentle to myself. "You can't heal from the same environment you are hurting." Getting stuck in negative thoughts and emotions was something I had to let go.

I was responsible for my own healing, and no one else. I knew that waiting for the person who put me into that situation to apologize may never happen, so I had to take charge of my healing. Allowing myself to lean on loved ones and their support was such a wonderful way of limiting isolation while also reminding me of the good things in my life. Speaking to a friend and having someone to share with was a relief and the assurance that all would be well, and I had a bright future ahead.

I was finally doing things I loved, engaging in community activities, women's forums, and church activities. Listening to testimonies of women who rose from nothing to something was one way that encouraged me to change my mindset. I had this urge for information, a hunger to go back to school and improve my status. I thank God for the opportunities that He opened for me.

Based on my experience from my first job (way back at the crusher), I was able to find work as a site clerk. I was intelligent, and my employer saw the potential in me. I received training opportunities that were fully paid for, my boss became my mentor, and I rose from the site clerk to a management-level position. I was able to not only support my son but also extend help to my family.

I will be forever grateful to that boss. I owe him what I am today. I later left that job and joined other organizations in the construction industry. I was engaged in local and international projects, excelling in whatever I did. I enrolled myself in college part-time and believe you me, I now run my own freelance business as a safety professional with different construction firms who request my services.

The many trainings I undertook improved my life. I was so committed to changing the narrative, which was evident to friends and employers alike. One time, I was committed to a different work appointment in the hospitality industry. The construction firm I worked for had a sister company running a chain of hotels in Kenya, we had no projects going, so I was temporarily reassigned.

I was given work in the purchasing and supplies department of the hotel chain. I am a fast learner, but how I became head of the department for the next five years is a mystery to me. Remember, this was a four-star hotel with many other branches across the country! Sometimes, it's not about the papers but the determination to learn and do your best.

I have grown more confident and stronger through my life's experiences. I believe that you can use your hurts as a lesson. Not only for yourself, but for others going through difficulties in life. I have mentored so many young mothers and single moms in general. I've also mentored young men and women pursuing occupational health and safety degrees from different universities, while never having stepped for into a university myself! I've started women's self-help groups among my friends and community that are still active today.

I am now a humanitarian, with global awards won for my work toward providing basic needs to orphans, vulnerable children, and widows. In 2020, I was inducted into the World Book of Greatness. I've been named a Sir Clyde Rivers family civility award winner, among many other international awards.

Through One Touch One Life, the organization I founded in 2010, I have been able to impact many lives, especially vulnerable children, orphans, and widows. Our community-based intervention program focuses on orphans and widows and was inspired by a young lady from the United Kingdom. She would sky dive to raise funds for orphaned children in Kenya. She also happened to be the daughter of my former boss in the hotel industry, which gave me the opportunity to accompany her to one of the orphanages to make a donation.

This was my first ever time visiting an orphanage, and it was my turning point. I discovered my calling and knew for sure that the visit was not a coincidence. That's where my passion for being a philanthropist began. Yes, I had my own storms, but that didn't stop me from following my trajectory.

The Bible says, "I can do all things through Christ who gives me strength," and for sure I have seen God make provisions for many projects. Without a single international donor, we've successfully built classrooms and dormitories, renovated homes, home makeovers for poor widows, and established school bursaries for needy children and sanitary towels projects for schools and villages.

I have been able to mobilize communities, church organizations, and corporations to support my dream of touching one life at a time. I can proudly say that the poor, naïve teenage mom is now a trail blazer. Not because she is wealthy or so learned, but because she identified her purpose through adversity and brought out the greatness within. We all have greatness within us!

To crown it all, I became a foster parent to one of the kids I first met in the first home I visited. He's now a grown man, a professional chef, and he calls me "mum." From the fear of raising one kid to a mother of many. All Glory to God. I learned one lesson: to be a philanthropist, you don't have to be rich, learned, or beautiful. You just need a heart that cares.

In life, we may not have gone through the same challenges, but we all may have trekked similar paths of life in different circumstances. A married woman who loses a spouse at an early age can be in an equally challenging situation, especially with kids to feed, no income, and no support system. A young woman forced into an early marriage just because she was pregnant only to later be abandoned with a child or children can be equally traumatized, especially if she had resigned her fate to being a housewife. With the bread winner gone, where does she start?

These scenarios are similar to the challenges that I went through and can lead to depression, loneliness, low self-esteem, financial burden, and a sense of guilt. Single parenting can plague an individual, sapping them of their energy, confidence, and happiness.

Your past doesn't determine your future. This is the message of my life. When I look back to where I came from and what I have achieved, it's a testimony. It's my hope that it will encourage someone reading this. My situation could have been different. I could have succumbed to negativity, self-pity, and given up on hope.

Your past, no matter how difficult it was, does not define your future. The choices we make and actions we take today will ultimately define who we become. Learn from your past and use the lessons to live a better life. When we honor the influence of our personal history, we benefit from the lessons that shaped who we are. Over the years, we develop, change, grow, and learn so many new things. Our interests, relationships, hobbies, and experiences change. If you stay stuck in the past, you will never truly be able to embrace who you are in the present day, and you will never be able to realize your potential.

When I was introduced into the World Book of Greatness, my name alongside so many high-key personalities made me realize that there's greatness within each one of us. The zeal to come out of the situation, repurposing my pain, and learning the lesson of what I went through has taught me that I can do all things through Christ who strengthens me.

Biography: Lucy Wairimu

Lucy Wairimu is a global humanitarian award winner and construction safety and health professional based in Nairobi, Kenya. She has been featured in both local and international media for the great work she is doing and has received many international awards and recognition under her nonprofit organization, One Touch One Life. This organization is registered in Kenya as an NGO with the Non-Governmental Organization Coordination Board.

Lucy has a passion for vulnerable children, widows, and single moms. Her dream is to work with volunteers worldwide to make a difference in Kanya.

Contact Lucy:
Info@onetouchonelife.or.ke
onetouchonelifeorg@gmail.com
WhatsApp: +254733783780, +254727068229, +254743617325
Facebook: Lucia Lucille Wairimu
https://www.linkedin.com/in/lucy-w-06b4ba35
www.onetouchonelife.or.ke
IG: Lucia Lucille
Skype: live:.cid.b0e4ab9b3d22bc8b_.

Looking for Me?

By Dr. Michelle Boone-Thornton

"No one man can, for any considerable time, wear one face to himself and another to the multitude without finally getting bewildered as to which is the true one." — Nathaniel Hawthorne

Have you ever thought about your life without that special person (a parent, sibling, or friend)? My brother Michael was my best friend ever since we were little.

He always came to my rescue. Yes, I was that child for whom no meant yes, stop meant proceed, and "let me think about it" meant a definite yes.

Whenever I jacked something up (and it was often), my brother made it right. At 18 years old, I stopped attending college, had an abortion, and started experimenting with drugs and alcohol. My life started spiraling out of control.

Michael swooped in and came to my rescue. He moved me to Northern Virginia with him. He helped me find a job in banking, and while shopping one day, I was approached by the store manager and asked to model the store's clothes. This led to other modeling opportunities and although I skipped the party scene, I continued to self-medicate with drugs and alcohol.

However, every once in a while, I would get a glimpse of some resemblance of the person I was meant to be. But soon, I realized this just made me a functional trainwreck. Yes, I said trainwreck. It felt as if a crash was imminent, like no matter what was happening, it felt like I was always on the edge of doom and gloom, and I couldn't shake it. Have any of you felt like this? With my success at work and with modeling, things seemed a little better, but this was nowhere near my happily ever after.

The truth is that I had just switched trains and went from riding one that was blazing down the track on the verge of barreling out of control to one that was traveling at maximum speed but still in the wrong direction.

During this period in my life, I started looking for myself in all the wrong places. I became **self-absorbed, selfish, self-centered**, and most of all, I took my brothers love for granted. It was not that I didn't love him, I just didn't know how to receive it or show it. I had erected walls for protection that no one could climb over or penetrate.

There were often times when I didn't have any idea who the real Michelle was. I looked happy and some would even comment that I was beautiful, but those were empty words that fell on a thorny heart. I didn't feel anything! Hearing those words about "self" just reinforced and reminded me of what others thought about me.

I would regularly overhear people saying it, and some would even tell me to my face, "You don't care about anyone but yourself." Somewhere beneath my pain, I knew my family loved me, but their love never registered as true and authentic. During that period in my life, I believed that it was out of obligation and staged for others to see. In a world where I was surrounded by people, I felt so alone all the time.

My brother received the newspaper daily at the apartment. The first section that I would read would be the obituaries. I think subconsciously I was looking for my name. Wanting to see what others said about me, who would miss me if I were no longer alive. You see, in the process of hiding my insecurities, doubt, worry, fear, and sadness from the world, I also choked out love, compassion, caring, happiness, and joy.

I was still on the train, and it was moving a little slower but still in the wrong direction. So, what did I do to stop the pain? I searched even harder for love. I moved back home, found a job, dated, married, and divorced. Never finding the love that I felt I deserved. During all this chaos, Michael was there with his unconditional love and support.

Ironically, people think that you must be homeless or hit rock bottom to experience hopelessness, but I learned that's not true. Throughout the shambles of my life, I had good jobs and was self-sufficient. I worked in a pharmacy and sold appliances, furniture, and cars. I worked in restaurants, retail, and banking, and it was all part of my search for the happiness that I saw in others.

At times, the unfulfillment left me in a state of hopelessness, desperation, and panic. I was growing older now and was still empty and alone. I poured everything into my job and began receiving accolades and rewards for my performance.

I married again, went back to college, and my twin daughters were born. I thought this is what every woman dreams of — a husband, home, children, family. But the void was still there, along with the doubt, shame, and guilt. I knew nothing about raising children, my first marriage was a total disaster, I had never really cared about anybody but myself.

I was so disappointed. I had worked so hard to become a woman that my family and others could be proud of, but again, I felt nothing but emptiness. How could I have been so disillusioned and end up on the same train? Although it was now going the speed limit, it was still headed in the wrong direction.

Michael was still there for me, but something was wrong, I could sense it. I knew all too well what hiding feelings and emotions looked like and felt like. How it kept your lungs from fully expanding, made your smile dim, and caused the light to stop short of reaching your face and from entering your mind, heart, body, and soul.

In 1993, Michael was diagnosed with HIV-AIDS. Today, with the advancements of modern medicine, people are living longer and are able to manage the disease with medication and other regimens. In the '90s, HIV-AIDS was a death sentence. Many were conflicted between sympathy for those infected and fear that the disease might spread to the general population. HIV-positive individuals were subjected to extreme levels of discrimination and stereotyped as gay. This led to homophobia and hatred toward anyone who contracted the disease. People were treated like lepers. They were stigmatized, socially devalued, ostracized, and shunned.

Have you ever felt like you just can't get a break? Nothing good happens to you, ever? This diagnosis felt like a sucker punch. The one person, the only person, who knew me, the good-bad, and indifferent, who understood me and loved me even when I did not love myself, was about to leave me. I could feel the pain of this loss welling up inside of me.

Inside I screamed and wailed like a wounded animal. I knew death was imminent and I was so confused and hurt. I thought, how could God let my brother board the same train I was on, moving fast and going in the wrong direction? After all, it was my name that I looked for in the obituaries daily, not his. My world was not only crashing down around me — it was exploding!

Things moved quickly after the diagnosis. Michael spent a short period in the hospital and then hospice. Hospice care started at my parent's house, then he was moved to a private care facility that was arranged through the Peninsula AIDS Foundation.

During this period, I struggled with sleep deprivation because every time I lay down and closed my eyes, I had to deal with the emotions that I kept bottled up inside and hidden from the world throughout the day. No one at my job knew my brother was dying. In fact, I did not share this information at all for fear that someone would ask what happened.

I didn't want people to judge him because he was such a good person. Inside my mind where my feelings were trapped, I love him unconditionally with every fiber of my being. **Do you hide from your feelings for fear that they might consume you?**

Do you find that you are more disappointed in yourself than others? I was so disappointed with myself for not being able to share my feelings with Michael even as he was beginning to transition from this world to the next. Just the shell of the person I knew lay dying. His body was ravished by a weakened immune system that left him wasting away with skeletal features that barely resembled the vibrant man I knew who loved life.

Each day, I saw remnants of the person I loved. His eyes longed to see the reciprocation of love from me, but I fought back the emotions, the tears, and the words. He left this world without ever hearing "I love you" from me. I had never felt numbness until his funeral. I was like some kind of automated version of myself saying the right words, greeting, and thanking everyone who attended.

On purpose, I did not read the obituaries from the day he died until months later. I felt like seeing his obituary would be the straw that would break me. It would keep me from putting one foot in front of the other as I carried the mountains of pain and hurt around like a chain around my neck. During this period the air seemed thinner, and my mind was unclear.

I know some of you reading my story can relate, and the truth is my narrative begins further back than where I started it for this publication. As a mental health provider, l now know that past childhood traumas that I buried and never addressed as I aged played a significant role in my ability to trust, care, and love. In this world, we will all experience some form of trauma, either directly or vicariously.

So, care for your mental health as you do your physical health. If this involves seeking professional help, then do so. The Bible encourages us, *Do not conform to the pattern of this world, but be transformed by the renewing of your mind. Then you will be able to test and approve what God's will is—his good, pleasing, and perfect will,* Romans 12:2 KJV.

It is my hope that others will learn from my story and not have to deal with some of the obstacles I experienced. But unfortunately, masking emotions is a learned behavior. It is rooted in cultural, societal, and family contexts. We are taught early on in life that we should always feel happy even when we are not, and yes — I wore a happy face for years.

I don't know about you, but I have always wondered why people who seemed so happy, who had everything to live for, would commit suicide. Well, although I never thought of taking my own life, there were times that I longed for death. I used self-talk to the point that I wondered about my own sanity.

I reminded myself that I was a mother and wife. I had people who needed me. I have always had people to lean on but not the trust to act on that need. But with Michael gone, I turned to my husband. After being stuck initially in the grief stages of denial, then anger, I began to move toward the light. The light that always seems to stop short of my face or penetrate my body.

I knew there I would find what I longed for. My mother had asked me to go clean out and pack Michael's house. For over a month, I made excuses not to go but my husband reassured me that he would go and be there to support me. If it became too difficult, he would take me home and complete the task alone.

As soon as I entered Michael's house, I was hit so hard with a wave of emotions that I threw up all over myself. My sobs quickly transformed into screams and fit of rage. My husband watched and gave me space to feel what I had been afraid to feel for months, years, and decades.

The guilt of holding back my feelings and telling my brother that I loved him came rushing out like a flood of raging waters. I finally collapsed on the steps, he put his arms around me, and I felt his love, I mean it was real. I didn't have to pretend to feel it.

After packing up his personal items and putting a few things out for trash pick-up, we left and went back to our home. The next day, I read Michael's obituary. I read the cards that were sent by family, friends, and co-workers. Everybody loved him and shared how he would be missed.

Instantly, I remembered how beautiful his funeral was, the words that were spoken, and the acts of kindness. For the first time in forever, I remembered the smile that came on my face.

What made it so special is that I didn't have to force it and the chain reaction of the grimace on the inside did not occur.

From Death to Renewal

By Dr. Michelle Boone-Thornton

"Seek out that particular mental attribute which makes you feel most deeply and vitally alive, along with which comes the inner voice that says, 'This is the real me.' When you have found that attitude, follow it." — William James

I began seeing glimpses of the person I longed for in me. After carefully examining my circumstances, I was surprised to find out that she (Michelle) had been there all along. Living out the helplessness and hopelessness that entrapped her and kept her from being able to receive (feel) or give (show) love.

I now understand the words "My Soul Cries Out." No one can hear these inaudible sounds. My soul was so tormented that my body ached for happiness, love, and fulfillment. I just never fought hard enough to move past the fear of rejection, worry, shame, doubt, and a hundred other emotions that I covered with layers of masks and erected walls to keep others out. I didn't understand that when you stop feeling, you cut God off, you stop dreaming, you stifle creativity, and you crush hope.

The mask and walls only reinforced the chains that kept me from being my authentic self. I like so many others tried to perfect myself (good wife, mom, employee, Sorors, daughter, community leader, church member) so that I could be found worthy of God's love. It took me a while to understand that because of my human frailties, I will never be perfect.

God told me in Psalm 82:6 that I am a child of God, and my Heavenly Father loves me. I slowly began to trust love and fight through the fears that held me back from being who God created me to be.

I do not know what took me so long to get to this place in my psyche. I do understand that it was my brother Michael's death that was the turning point in my life. I still regret not telling him how much I loved him before he died. But I know in my heart that he knew. I could have easily buried myself along with all the emotions that I kept hidden from the world.

I experienced the dichotomy of being both present (broken) and absent (buried) at the same time. But I have a praying husband who prayed for me when I didn't know how to pray for myself. I had an "Aunt Boose," Elizabeth Brock, who prayed for me daily and took me to church and sat me on the mourners bench every summer I visited her until she passed. Her prayers from the grave saved me.

My brother Michael showed me what love, family, and friendship looked like. He always encouraged and believed in me even when I did not believe in myself. Each one of them — husband, aunt, brother provided the anchor that I needed to keep me connected to God. The act of accepting Michael's death forced me to put down my walls and unmask long enough to feel the presence of God and experience His all-consuming love. I was at a point in my life where my soul was tired of the ongoing fight and struggle in my mind.

My parents raised me in church. but like the lyrics of Shirley Caesar's song, I was "playing church" and now all I could do was call on the name of Jesus. Oh, what a friend we have in Jesus!! I was taught to be strong, but it was in my weakest moment that God stepped in. I invite each reader to let God into your life, now!

I am so grateful that we serve a God of second chances. In my case second, third, twentieth, and forty-eighth chances. In other words, He's not counting. He waited for me to show up long enough to enter my life. I no longer questioned whether I was loved. If fact, the closer I got to becoming my authentic self, the more I could feel my husband's love, my children's love, and the love of others.

I decided to go back to college and finish my bachelor's degree, and shortly afterward, my son was born. I completed my master's and doctorate. I was heavily influenced by the people I worked with at the AIDS Foundation, so I decided to pursue degrees in social work, counseling, and educational psychology. I have worked in the field of mental health for over 25 years and spent eight years in higher education. If you are reading this, and this resonates with you, just know you have the power to change the direction of your train (life).

You must release the negative, traumatic, hurtful events, situations, and circumstances that happened in your past. These atrocities keep you bound and unable to move forward. I could not get my train (life) moving in the right direction until I let go. I will admit that I was so scared to let people in until I exercised faith over fear. You may ask, what does that involve? Well, it means that I was scared but I did it anyway. I knew that I could not continue living in the dark. My world was so dark that I couldn't find myself, my true authentic self.

As a professor, I always summarize my lectures into steps and key components. This helps with recall and one's ability to align new information with pre-existing concepts and ideas, here are a few:

- Learn to love yourself first, which will teach you how to love others.
- It is second nature to mask emotions but give yourself permission to feel (not just go through the motions) the good, bad, and indifferent.
- Don't pressure yourself to be perfect. I wasted too much of my life trying to be (and in fear of not being) the perfect wife, mother, sister, daughter, etc.
- Life is a gift, so recognize God's gifts while you have them.
- Invest in yourself, discover yourself, embrace yourself, and be true to yourself.
- Celebrate who you are, where you are in life, and what's to come.

Yes, I experienced some trials and tribulations, but the truth of the matter is, if I had to do it all over again, I would not change a thing. I know that sounds strange, but my journey shaped me into the person that I am today! I have used every moment of my existence as preparation for my journey as an international speaker, author, educator, coach, and mentor. I use these platforms to deliver a message to help people worldwide release the emotional baggage they've been masking for years by living life more abundantly and open to a God who can Refill and Renew them with love and peace, allowing them to fulfill their God-given purpose.

In my workshops, I create a safe space for attendees to think about and explore their emotions. Healing begins person by person, group by group, organization by organization, and beyond. God has guided me in writing a three-book series that reinforces my presentations and workshops. It allows me to provide the tools to help people understand and identify masking in their own lives and write about buried painful occurrences that they hide from the world with invisible masks and walls for protection.

Unfortunately, in a world of click, point, drag, and take a pill, there is no quick fix, medication, or surgery for a broken heart, broken trust, broken childhoods, and broken relationships. These events produce traumatic responses, feelings, and emotions and it takes work to undo what's been done over time.

Renew. This concept is vital to our very being. We must renew our thoughts each day (Romans 12:2) We can easily get caught up in negative thinking patterns. In fact, when something happens, we usually think of the worst. It is human nature. **Have you experienced a time in your life when you felt stuck?**

Nothing bad is happening and at the same time, nothing good is happening either. We can enter a state of autopilot and start to think this is it, this is all there is for me in this life. By renewing your mind, you give yourself a fresh start and a reset. You welcome more positive and hopeful thoughts. You can see the good in things that once looked impossible or fruitless.

You replace doom and gloom with intentionality. A vital part of renewing your mind is perspective. View things from a perspective of gratitude. Most importantly, a renewed mind is full of hope. You no longer see yourself as a victim but as a victor. The obstacles in our lives can become opportunities to grow, learn, and develop.

In my workshops, I always leave my attendees with hope and an intervention. Readers, this is a key component of overcoming a defeatist mindset!

I keep a gratitude journal and would suggest that you do the same. When I initially started writing my daily entries, I thanked God for all that I had, my husband, my children, family, friends, and all other important relationships, places that I have visited, and things that He has provided, home, cars, education, etc.

Now, I also thank God for my journey. What I went through qualifies me to help others. I have met all walks of people as a speaker and author and there are some who ask, "What makes Dr. Boone-Thornton an expert on the topic of wearing masks?" and I just smile and think *you don't have time to hear about how I made it over!!*

People are people and they will question your authority. Just remember that elevation and promotion come from God and not from people, so you stand wherever God plants you!! Psalm 75:6-7 KJV.

Biography: Dr. Michelle Boone-Thornton

Dr. Michelle Boone-Thornton is an educator, international speaker, author, trainer, and coach. She has championed education from kindergarten through college and has spoken at venues and conferences all over the U.S. and aboard. Dr. Boone-Thornton combines her 25 years in the field of mental health with the joy of teaching to help people improve their emotional wellbeing, discover their purpose, uncover gifts and talents, and connect with their true authentic self.

Dr. Boone-Thornton holds a bachelor's in social work, master's in urban education guidance and counseling, and doctorate from Regent University in educational psychology with a concentration in research. Dr. Boone-Thornton's is certified through the Commonwealth of Virginia as a Qualified Mental Health Provider (QMHP) with a specialization in children and adolescents. As a practitioner, she has provided direct, supervisory, and administrative services in mental health working in residential, community-based, and juvenile court programs throughout Virginia and Alabama.

Dr. Boone-Thornton currently works in higher education. She has served in many capacities, as the associate chair of an undergraduate program, director of a doctorate program, as an adjunct, assistant, associate, and tenured professor. Her published book series, *Transforming Your Reality Removing the Mask*, book-chapters, journal articles, and bulletins that she has authored reflect her interest in education, mental health, and emotional wellbeing.

She has published and presented in Nairobi, Kenya (2022) and Madrid, Spain (2019). Dr. Boone-Thornton has received numerous awards for her work, but her most prestigious award to date was the I Can Change Nations Astell Collins Global Inspiration Award as a Generation Leader (2022) for recognition of her work with current and aspiring business leaders in Nairobi, Kenya. In 2023, she received The NANBWPC National Sojourner Truth Meritorious Service Award for community service.

God will restore! Deuteronomy 30:3 (NLT)

drmichelleboonethornton.com

https://www.linkedin.com/in/drbt

Things Fall Apart
By Deborah Robinson

"Therefore, what God has united and joined together, man must not separate [by divorce]" – Mark 10:9 AMP

"When we met, I always knew
I would feel the magic for you
On my mind constantly
In my arms is where you should be
I love you here by me, baby
You let my love fly free
I want you in my life for all time
I'm caught up in the rapture of love
Nothing else can compare
When I feel the magic of you
Aaahhhhhhh" – Anita Baker

We met at Virginia State University, where I was a freshman, and he was a junior. It was a cool fall evening, and the crisp night air was invigorating. The brothers of the Omega Psi Phi fraternity had performed in front of the cafeteria and the crowd was electrified! The brothers' energy was contagious. People were cheering and dancing along as they stomped the pavement and moved in unison.

I was walking back to the dormitory with friends, laughing and chatting about the performance, when he walked over to me and asked, "Are you Melvin Lewis's niece?" I responded, "Yes, are you Wanda's brother?" We were both from large families, and our families had known each other for years. It was only a matter of time before we fell in love. This is our story of love, loss, and redemption. It's a story of hope, and it's a story of second chances.

After that night of introductions, he would stop by the dormitory occasionally. He lived off-campus with roommates in a two-story colonial style house. During the spring semester, he invited me over for dinner one evening. Not long afterwards, his small bedroom became our haven. It was a place where we could be ourselves, where we could laugh and love without judgment. After the spring semester, we returned to our respective homes, only five blocks away from each other. We would take long walks in the park and reminisce about school days, house parties, high school jams, our favorite songs, and talk about our plans for the future.

Some days he'd convince me to ride my bike to his house while everyone was away. He was contemplating joining the Navy at the time, and I had plans to move to New York. We were both excited about the possibilities, but we were also a little bit scared. The new school year approached, and we found ourselves back at Virginia State, in new dorms and with a newfound freedom. We were no longer bound by our parents' rules, and we were free to explore our relationship without any restrictions. We were in love, and we were excited to see what the future held.

One year away from home and into my second year in college, I was wearing a button that read, "I'm not fat, I'm pregnant." It was my way of avoiding the questions that came laced with judgment. I was keenly aware of my insufficiency, but I was determined to succeed. I would survive just as my predecessors had. I had grown up in a community where single motherhood was not only frowned upon, but also shamed. We embraced our pregnancy and accepted the responsibility of parenthood. I wanted to love this child like I had not been loved. I wanted this man to love. I had a family of my own to love.

We dropped out of college to support our family. He reported to Navy boot camp, while I continued my studies at Virginia State until my doctor put me on bedrest. Our firstborn graced this planet in the spring of '88. While he was away, I prepared for our new life together. I rented a quaint, two-bedroom apartment and furnished it with my favorite pieces: an old headboard that I had refinished, and a wicker furniture set I had purchased while in high school.

I spent hours writing letters to him and crafting gifts to keep him amused. I enjoyed our telephone conversations, and each one left me in anticipation of the next. I cherished those moments. When he finally came home, I was overjoyed. I was excited to start our new life together, knowing that we would face challenges but also knowing that we would overcome them together.

He was gleaming with pure joy and pride as he held our baby girl for the first time. He couldn't believe that this little person was his, and he was excited to start this new journey as a father. I was excited and relieved that he would be by my side for the duration. It seemed to have been the longest six months of my life. We were married at the ages of 20 and 23, he being three years my senior. We were married at our church on August 25, 1988, after a few weeks of "couple's counseling." With my baby on my hip and my tall glass of water by my side, I had all the love I needed in the world. He was the perfect man for me and in him I saw no flaws. I felt like I had found my soulmate.

Two years later, our second bundle of joy was born. She was a wise child with eyes that seemed to peer into your soul. She had her father's dimples and every night he rocked her to sleep. When we got pregnant the second time, we were living with my great grandmother. He stayed with his brother some nights and I was suspicious of his behavior. Shortly after our second beautiful baby girl was born, we rented a small two-bedroom flat with a view of the lake.

But things began to change all too soon. One night, he did not come home from work. I panicked. I had been praying all through the night. The death of Black men by police brutality and street crimes had been a part of my life's story, and I was only 22 years old. When he arrived that morning, I felt a wave of relief wash over me. The nerve endings in my body that had been on edge all night began to slowly relax. I was relieved that he was alive and unharmed.

I forgave him, but the wounds of past betrayals were slowly opening. I was devastated and untrusting, always waiting for the other shoe to drop. I thought I knew what it would take to sustain us, but I had no idea of the magnitude of what we were up against.

We attended church, as that was the only way we could or would survive in my mind. Although we were together, I felt rejected and the feelings of being unworthy of his love fueled my resentment toward my husband. I kept hearing that "a man will be a man" and that I had to accept it. At the time, I did what was commonplace for most women: suck it up. I wasn't in an abusive relationship, my husband "loved" me; therefore, I should put my feelings aside. "It's not about you," someone said. Translation to my heart: *You are not worthy, you are not worthy of love, and especially not the love you desire.*

I may have acquiesced for a while, but resentment and pain grow into bitterness when left unattended. I rebelled and did things my way. I struggled with forgiveness and insecurity. Instead of seeking healing, I acted out of pain. We argued and were both reckless. I lost trust and felt we were better off apart. Things were bad between us. We were hanging out with friends, going to clubs, and spending more time away from home instead of spending time with each other.

Our relationship grew progressively worse. I finally found the strength to ask for a separation. I knew it would be difficult, but I was determined to make a change. I planned a trip to New York to celebrate my birthday and promised myself that things would be different when I returned. There had been constant fighting, blaming, and infidelity.

I was exhausted, both physically and emotionally. I felt like I was drowning, and I needed to get out of the water. I asked for a separation. I defied the expectation of remaining in a marriage unwanted, unloved, and unappreciated by my husband, so the only alternative was divorce.

When my husband moved out, I decided I was no longer pretending. The shoe was on the other foot. I was in an extramarital affair that eventually severed our relationship. We continued to fight each other with our words and deeds, causing further damage to our children and family. It's funny how society defames women for the same transgressions for which men are rewarded. He told me that I had the "Scarlet Letter A" on my forehead. I rejected it in the moment, but I wore it like a tattoo for years.

When a woman commits adultery, she is shamed, but a man is given accolades. I was ashamed of what I had done, but like Hester Prynne, I was angry about the double standard. Women are expected to live in the shame, blame, and guilt of their mistakes. They are shamed by their partners and worse, shamed by women in their community with whom they should find refuge. A wise woman understands the power of healing herself so that her family, community, and the world beyond can be healed. More importantly, she understands that we are called to heal through love and compassion. This is how we change generations.

But at that time, I wore the shame and his words kept playing in my mind. I was told by another woman that my time was over. Really? I wasn't 30 years old yet. I showed up among family and friends feeling like I didn't belong. I suffered from performance orientation. If I perform, then others will accept and love me. I accepted roles that others placed on me instead of defining myself. I was insecure, and I didn't realize just how deeply wounded I'd been. I even hid in church because I didn't want to be "found out." If I didn't commit to anything, I wouldn't be exposed.

In hindsight, I realize I was harboring bitterness and judgment not only from the infidelity, but deep hurt and trauma that I brought into the relationship. After all, we were both out of covenant and out of the will of God. However, my assignment is to share my story and be accountable for my decisions in hopes that someone else may be healed.

Our divorce was finalized in 1998. We shared joint custody of our daughters. They visited their father every other weekend and during the summer. That same year, my daughters led me back to my first love, Christ. I like to think of it this way: I gave them life, and they saved my life. One Sunday after church, my eldest daughter said she wanted to be baptized.

The following Sunday, both daughters answered the call for water baptism. This was the same altar where we had stood 10 years prior with our firstborn and vowed to be together in sickness and in health, for better or worse. We celebrated their dedication with family and friends over dinner. It was a glorious day, the sun was shining brightly, and I was filled with joy about their decision to follow Christ. From that day forward, my life began to change.

I was growing in my faith and devoting more time to prayer. During this time, one of my colleagues became instrumental in my spiritual growth. Through our friendship, I learned more about God, His love for me, and how to live a more Christ-like life. She is a devoted Christian woman, Sunday School teacher, and deaconess. I am still grateful for her friendship and influence on my spiritual journey. We talked for hours about biblical stories, salvation, and the Full Gospel.

I remember attending a conference at the local coliseum in our city where a well-known bishop taught on covenant relationships. He explained that too often, two broken people come together in hopes that the other is equipped to "fix" them or is somehow responsible for the other's happiness. He also explained the importance of being made whole in Christ before entering into a covenant relationship (marriage) and creating a family. The emphasis on being made whole was outstanding as it suggests that many of us are broken until we allow God to make us whole. Salvation is only one step, however; the process of being made whole in a fallen world is another.

I had been in church all of my life and didn't realize there was so much more to salvation. Somewhere deep within, I knew I wasn't going to hell for my sins, but I didn't know about this abundant life filled with joy and peace until I began to study the Word of God. I was so intrigued and inspired by his teaching because I had never heard the Scriptures taught in that manner. I began to see things differently and develop a new perspective.

I was attending a local junior college at the time and for the first time in a long time, I felt empowered. I was learning to enjoy my own company and the beauty of being with myself rather than what I had previously considered "alone." I took myself to dinner, to the movies, and didn't need the companionship of others to fill the space. At first it seemed strange, but I loved it, and that was all that mattered.

On May 18, 2002, equipped with this newfound love for myself and falling deeper in love with God, I packed up my belongings and moved to Greensboro, North Carolina to attend Bennett College. I had received one of their largest scholarships from the UNCF the prior year, but my plans were deferred due to the terrorist attacks on 9/11. I had always dreamed of living in a small town, and I was excited to start a new chapter in my life.

As you might imagine, the conversation about moving to North Carolina with my ex-husband was not easy. He was concerned about the distance and the fact that we did not have a support system in North Carolina. The girls lived with him for the remainder of the school year and summer, then joined me in August, just in time for school. Some family members and friends thought I had lost my mind. They couldn't understand why I would leave my family in Richmond. But I knew in my heart that this was the right decision for me and my daughters. I had been struggling for a long time.

But then, something happened. I started to fall in love with myself. I realized that I was worthy of love and happiness, and that I didn't need to rely on anyone else to make me happy. At the same time, I was spending more time in prayer and listening for direction from God. I felt a connection to Him that I had never felt before. I felt like He was guiding me and helping me to find my way.

When I moved to Greensboro, it was like a breath of fresh air. I met new people who accepted me for who I was. I found a church home where I felt connected to God and my community. I started to feel more confident and empowered than ever before. In Greensboro, I found my place in the world. I found my community. I found my family. And I found my faith. I was grateful for the opportunity to start over and to create a new life for myself and my daughters.

My spirit soared in Greensboro. I felt like I was finally living my best life. My daughters and I were received by some of the most loving, dedicated, God-fearing people I have ever met. Our Bishop and First Lady were transparent, filled with the wisdom of God, and they possessed a natural gift of compassion to father and mother the congregation. I attended Bible college, church conferences, prayer shut-ins, Bible study, and for the first time, I felt like I could finally be myself.

There was something within me that shifted. I was on the path to a better life, but I still felt trapped. I was experiencing joy and satisfaction, but I was still holding onto unforgiveness. I knew that I needed to let go of the past in order to move forward.

The litmus test for unhealed wounds is telling the same old story. And I was still telling the story of my pain. I was fortunate to have met a group of women who were also on a journey of healing. Through our shared experiences, I learned the importance of forgiveness and the power of prayer.

One of the most memorable experiences of my journey was our participation in a corporate fast to break generational curses. Our bishop led us through a training on generational curses and then we fasted and prayed for three days. During that time, God revealed patterns within my family that He was breaking. He also promised to restore the years that had been stolen (Joel 2:25).

If you are struggling with unforgiveness or generational curses, I encourage you to seek out a community of believers who can walk with you on your journey. Together, you can break the chains of the past and experience the freedom that God has for you. I knew that something was about to change in my life. I could feel a stirring, a restlessness, a calling.

As we prepared to send our eldest daughter off to college and planned our youngest daughter's sweet 16 party, my ex-husband and I began to open up to each other. We had long since asked for forgiveness — a sign of growth. We weren't the same people anymore. Our lives had changed, and we had matured in many ways. Our conversations were different; our communication with each other was different. We were listening to each other without judgment.

One evening, I was speaking with a college friend. As usual, before we ended the call, she asked about my ex-husband. She had encouraged me to hang out with him while we were in college and knew our history together. I told her that we had been in conversation lately and while she was talking, I heard the Lord say, "You never asked Me what My will for your marriage was." I almost threw the phone on the floor! What? I knew that I had not listened to God concerning our marriage. I told my friend what I'd heard, and she encouraged me to gift him a Bible. I did. Unbeknownst to me at that time, my circumstances would change drastically. I had been praying the "search my heart" prayer for some time and heard so many people say that you'd better be ready when you ask God to search your heart.

But I was ready for a change. I desired a heart of forgiveness, trust, and love. I knew that I wasn't perfect, but God had begun a good work in me, and I was committed to seeing it through. Besides, who would be better to show me myself than my Creator? I started by forgiving people who had hurt me and asking for forgiveness from those I had hurt. It wasn't easy but I knew it was necessary for my own healing. I was trusting God more, even when I didn't understand what He was doing.

"For my thoughts are not your thoughts, neither are your ways my ways, saith the Lord. For as the heavens are higher than the earth, so are my ways higher than your ways, and my thoughts than your thoughts" (Isaiah 55:8-9). I was working full-time in real estate sales when the economy shifted. My real estate career had just begun two years prior to the housing market crash. I was meeting new people, networking with industry

professionals, and enjoying the financial rewards. I had purchased a townhome in a new community that we loved.

The housing crisis impacted my income significantly. Lenders were being shut down, and buyers were afraid to purchase. I accepted a full-time position with my former employer and several months later accepted a position with a different department.

It had been a struggle to catch up with household bills when the market tanked, and I needed to make a decision. I considered selling our townhome and put it on the market. There were no offers after a few weeks. Each morning, my daughter and I prayed together before leaving the house for the day as it had been our custom when the three of us were living together. My eldest daughter was in college at the time.

One morning in particular, my daughter prayed that we listen to God for His will concerning the house and not our own. I took the house off the market and waited for God to reveal His plan. I was anxious. I couldn't hear clearly because I was constantly thinking of what I could do to sustain us. I contemplated filing for bankruptcy. I experienced a series of setbacks, but the straw that broke the camel's back was a car accident in which my car was totaled, and I had just made the final payment. I filed for bankruptcy.

Now, I realize that these are everyday life occurrences. When the housing market crashed and I lost my job as a real estate agent, I picked up a 9-5. Millions of people around the world were affected by the crash, and I was one of them. It was hard to stay positive, but I knew that I had to keep going. It seemed to be a snowball effect, one thing after the next.

In a conversation with my ex-husband, I told him that I was considering moving back home to Virginia. He offered to assist me financially, and I was grateful for the offer, but I needed to weigh my options. We continued to communicate, and his visits became more frequent. Leaving our home after a day visit, he held my hand and said, "I want my wife back." We talked more and I prayed that God would reveal His will.

I had been contemplating what all of this meant and how our relationship would be mended after all these years. What would our children think, or how would this impact them if we really weren't prepared to bring the relationship and family back together? What would others think about us being together again? I felt as if my circumstances were pushing me home.

I prayed and shared my heart with two women I trusted. They both agreed to fast with me as I sought the Lord. I asked God if I should pursue our relationship, marriage, and family. The word of the Lord came to me on May 6, 2007, during Sunday worship service: *"Pursue and you shall recover all, and without fail"* – I Samuel 30:8. Lord, I need another sign. Clearly my thoughts are not like Yours.

It wasn't enough that God had answered immediately and succinctly considering I had specifically asked if I should pursue. I had only been in my new position for a few months when I was called into a meeting with the rest of the team. Our directors announced that the clinical departments would be closed indefinitely across the country. And just like that, I was laid off. The move home was confirmed by the layoff.

Our youngest daughter graduated a couple months later in June, and during the weekend of July 4th, 2008, my ex-husband rented a truck, loaded our belongings, and drove it back to Richmond. I arrived the next day and was greeted with our favorite meal, oven fried chicken and a vanilla cake with chocolate icing, as a welcome home surprise. *"Behold, I will do a new thing, now it shall spring forth; shall you not know it? I will even make a road in the wilderness and rivers in the desert"* (Isaiah 43:19).

Redeeming Love

By Deborah Robinson

I will restore to you the years that the locust hath eaten, the cankerworm, and caterpillar, and the palmerworm, my great army which I sent among you. – Joel 2:25-26 KJV

The second time around held its challenges. After a few years, I realized he was not ready to sever ties with some relationships. In fact, he was not ready to commit. Once we were back together, we found ourselves facing challenges from our past. Our actions were reminiscent of past behaviors that triggered certain negative responses. But we continued to communicate and talk about what we were feeling. This time around, we were listening to each other.

Sometimes, our past judgments of each other influenced our present circumstances. There were times that I questioned God's plan. Either I had not heard from God, or I had unrealistic expectations of our relationship. I was looking at our situation rather than trusting God's plan. I felt hypocritical and worried that things were falling apart rather than being restored. Had I made a mistake moving to Richmond?

But if I had misunderstood God's instructions, why hadn't He interrupted my steps? Who was I to dictate to God how to restore my marriage and family? God had not promised to fulfil His plan on my timeframe. Additionally, there is this notion that there are no consequences for our actions once we have come to repentance. A victim's trauma does not magically fade away simply because he or she has forgiven the perpetrator. No, there are consequences for our actions and decisions. What God said to me was, "Go back to your place of pain and submit."

I thought it would be easy because I had done the work of inner reflection, repentance, and forgiveness. But this reunion was by Divine Design. We were growing in our relationship. He knew me intimately, my flaws, insecurities, strengths, and desires, but was not aware of my triggers. The same is true for me. I was not aware of some of his triggers. We came back into the relationship with assumptions from our past. Some of those assumptions were that we fully understood things about each other when in fact, there were things about ourselves, individually, that we did not understand.

This was a new level of healing. The foundation for this chapter of my life had been laid. In God's wisdom and timing, He revealed that He was growing deep roots within us both. When a seed is planted, there are several steps that must take place before that seed fully manifests. The seed must be planted, watered, have just the right exposition to the sun, and given time to grow – seed, time, and harvest.

There are certain conditions that must be present for the seed to germinate. First, the soil in which it is planted must be cultivated. The planter must be careful not to overwater the crop because the seed will rot, and insufficient watering will cause the seed to dry up. The Word of God is a seed planted in our hearts.

When the Word is received in our cultivated hearts, it is planted on good ground. It will take root and manifest God's promise. Beware, it is tempting to pull up the seed before it has fully developed. Because we cannot see the roots, which represent God's work in our lives, we may pull it up or curse it with our words before the promise comes to fruition. "Let us not become weary in doing good, for at the proper time we will reap a harvest if we do not give up" (Galatians 6:9-10, NIV).

God was working underneath the surface to grow our relationship stronger than before, not only for us, but for His glory. You cannot see what God is doing, nor is it measured by status, money, assets, notoriety, class, or education. All of that can change in one moment, by one decision. God is always working, molding, shaping, and changing our hearts to demonstrate the kind of love He desires versus the love we understand with the carnal mind. He is taking us to deeper depths!

Regardless of what I felt during those times, I continued to hold on to God's promises. God was moving us forward. I had grown in many areas, but I had grown as a single mother raising my daughters, not as a wife. What more did God require of me? After all, I left my home, family, everything I owned, and moved to Greensboro. I had gone to Bible college. I fasted, prayed, and believed God to break generational curses in my family. My faith had increased, and I was not the same. This was a move of God! I saw lives and circumstances change through prayer.

Certainly, God knew that we would encounter these issues once we were together. But God was doing a deeper work within me, and my obedience was not transactional. God was not interested in the sacrifices I had made in the past. He was interested in my heart and the transformation that was taking place between us and in our family. Hallelujah!

God reminded me that when I prayed and asked if I should pursue my family, He said, "Pursue and surely you shall recover all and without fail." Some days, I would release it all to God, and other days, when I was alone with my own thoughts, I would take matters into my own hands. This comes as no surprise because many of us Holy Ghost-filled women of God do this every day. I trusted God for other people, encouraged them, and believed God would move on their behalf.

But somewhere within, I did not believe God fully for the secret pray of my heart. I did not fully believe He would do the same for me. I continued to stand on God's Word. I changed my prayer asking God to help my unbelief. I asked the Father to reveal those things that were hidden in the recesses of my heart. God began to show me those areas at the root of my belief system that were causing me to doubt Him and not trust the process.

I had no awareness of generational curses or patterns when we first married. During my spiritual journey in Greensboro, God revealed the generational patterns in my family lineage: drugs, alcoholism, adultery, incarceration, divorce, and teenage pregnancy. My grandmother had her first child at age 16. My mother had me at age 16. I had my firstborn at age 19, and my youngest daughter had her first child at age 19. I'm guessing by now that you see the pattern. Generational patterns are like spiderwebs. You realize they exist but can never discern that you have come into contact with one until you walk through it. Generational curses take us out of the will of God and more importantly, out of fellowship with God.

Because they are *generational*, we think of those patterns as normal and place more value on what is familiar than God. We align ourselves with the pattern rather than aligning with God's Word. Physicians refer to them as our "family history." Notice how some medical professionals, not all, prematurely prescribe treatments based on family history rather than devising a treatment plan to change the learned behavior at the root of the chronic illness? Until generational patterns are exposed and challenged, we will find ourselves caught in the spiderweb. Stay with me.

Some generational patterns bring shame, guilt, and emotional and financial insecurity that influence our inner belief systems. Our inner belief systems fuel our capacity for self-love, self-respect, and self-worth. What I understood later in life is that we were both broken coming into the relationship. Many, but not all, of our life's choices and experiences were impacted by generational patterns. Those patterns shaped our beliefs, perspectives, and self-awareness. At some point in life, we have a responsibility to know what is in our hearts and to allow God to heal it. Ultimately, we decide if we will continue those destructive generational patterns or change the trajectory of our legacy. This requires healing work. Let's go deeper.

Oftentimes, people will not do the work to heal themselves because they lack the tools, resources, or knowledge. They don't know where to start. I had an awakening that thrust me into counseling. We don't know what we don't know. Moreover, accepting responsibility for the pain we have caused others is painstakingly difficult. When I asked God to search me and know my heart, I desired the truth about myself. We all have said, "Well, God knows my heart." But what about the remainder of that same verse? *"And see if there be any wicked way in me and lead me in the way of everlasting."* That requires courage. God revealed the wicked ways and darkness of my heart and brought me to repentance.

My soul was sorrowful. There was sorrow, pain, discord, and death from my childhood that I carried into adulthood. I grew up in an environment of depression and anxiety, another generational pattern. It seemed to have taken on a personality or shadow in my life that kept me waiting for the other shoe to fall. There was a sense that people and things were taken away from me; therefore, I had trust issues.

I knew that I was not living life to the fullest, but I didn't know how to describe or shake this feeling that seemed ever-present through the highs and lows of life. There was a fear that I had accepted in childhood. And though I would speak God's Word over my life, that cloud of fear would creep into my mind causing me to doubt the very promises of God. The secrets, coping mechanisms, and vows that kept me through the early adulthood season of my life would no longer suffice. God is calling us higher!

God continued to reveal the issues of my heart. As I mentioned before, my spirit had soared Greensboro, but my soul was dry. When I saw within myself the pain that I had caused my husband, my daughters, and our extended family, without excusing and blaming, I think I cried for three years. This was what I called the dark night of my soul. My prayer went from "Search me, oh God" to "Oh, what a wretched man I am, who will deliver me from the body of this death?" (Romans 7:24-25).

When I began to pray this prayer with sincere conviction and an overwhelming desire to be made whole, I was aware that there had been unresolved issues in my life. *"Call to Me and I will answer you, and tell you [and even show you] great and mighty things, [things which have been confined and hidden], which you do not know and understand and cannot distinguish"* (Jeremiah 33:3, AMP).

My ex-husband and I had asked for each other's forgiveness in the distant past. We had done so on separate occasions. Asking for forgiveness signified growth and a willingness to take ownership of our actions, decisions, and behaviors. In my mind, the acknowledgement and acceptance of forgiveness constituted a release from our covenant. Our marriage had been dissolved in the natural sense through human laws; however, the spiritual covenant between us and God had not. I had never felt released in that way.

Much to my surprise, God was not only restoring my extended family, but He was also restoring the family to which I had given birth. The healing of my soul would take place in the environment in which my pain was caused. It was also taking place in the environment in which I had caused pain.

Our God will perfect the things that concern His people. We can rest assured that God will cover our transgressions, but there are consequences for our decisions and actions – cause and effect. When there is a breach in the marriage covenant, trauma is inevitable on some level because the breach involves souls. And although they insist that they always felt loved by both parents, our daughters were deeply impacted, especially our youngest. If you are a young woman or man reading my story today and can relate in some way, please seek wise counsel before making a decision to dissolve your marriage and tear your family apart. If you are reading this book, you have resources and tools to make better choices. I walked away from God and my values.

Our oldest daughter has many fond memories of love and good times about our marriage. But our youngest daughter readily recalls the arguing, fighting, and discord. Our eldest carries the joy and love of our union in her spirit. However, our youngest internalized the anxiety and broken heart I experienced while she was in my womb. When she was old enough to speak, she did not — she observed.

Her recollection of our relationship is connected to the inner turmoil she experienced in utero. She describes it as

155

having been long on a downward spiral by the time of our divorce. It had begun while she was in my womb. Think about the conditions in which they were born. One marinated in a womb of love, joy, unity, and longing. The other marinated in betrayal, despair, and insecurity. Again, there are parts of this testimony that are not for everybody, but only YOU. Generational patterns and behaviors can be traced to the womb – in utero.

The chemical balance, imbalance, harmony, and stress from a mother is passed along to the infant. This is one reason why two children can come from the same womb, grow up in the same environment, and have different perspectives, lives, and world views. It is why it is imperative to heal traumatic experiences and adverse childhood experiences (ACEs) before entering into covenant relationships.

The cycle is repeated as children are exposed to these patterns because the children take them into adulthood as normal behaviors. Lies, inner vows, and false expectations become a part of the inner belief system. They are passed down, nurtured in our hearts, and manifested in families. Again, it is our responsibility to know the issues of our hearts and allow God to heal as He reveals. "Guard your heart above all else, for it determines the course of your life" (Proverbs 4:23). It determines your consequences.

Sometimes it takes years to accept the truth, do the work, and walk in the manifested promises of God. Yes, God is a promise keeper, He cannot lie. The question is whether I truly believed God would manifest those promises in my life. And even more important, what was the cause of my doubt and unbelief regarding the secret prayers of my heart? Matthew 11:24 says, "For this reason I am telling you, whatever things you ask for in prayer [in accordance with God's will], believe [with confident trust] that you have received them, and they will be given to you." But I must first believe. If there are hidden lies in my belief system, it will hinder my belief in God's promises to me! Healing work is critical to changing our belief system, our relationships, and living an abundant life!

There were unhealed places in my life and my ex-husband's life that were hindering us from taking the next step to marriage. What I wanted from my ex-husband was a commitment to trust God in the process. His relationship with God had to be on his own terms, so I waited. I was so excited when he started attending church with me on Sundays. He even joined the Men's Bible Study, which caught me by surprise. I could tell that God was working in his life, and I was proud to see him growing closer to Him.

After Sunday service, we would often talk about the message and how God had spoken to us individually. These conversations were enriching for me, and I always felt uplifted and encouraged afterwards. He had such a deep understanding of the Bible, and he was always able to offer me wise insights and guidance. I had forgotten that he obtained his graduate degree from a faith-based college while I was living in North Carolina. This only made me love him more, knowing that he had such a strong foundation in his faith. I was grateful for his spiritual growth, and I couldn't wait to see what God had in store for him.

One Sunday, following prayer ministry workshop, my ex-husband poured out his heart. I knew something had shifted the day before, but I wasn't sure to what level. This was different. He shared that God had been dealing with his heart regarding our relationship for some time and that he had been grappling with unforgiveness. A few weeks later, after receiving my father's blessings, he proposed. Our daughters were with us that evening. There was an indescribable joy between all of us that night. This time, we planned to celebrate our nuptials surrounded by family and friends in the fall of 2020. After 12 long years, we were finally closing the old chapter and moving forward.

COVD-19 and the pandemic thwarted our plans, but we refused to let it derail our love. We decided to hold our wedding at a beautiful park overlooking our city. We had two weeks to pull this off if we were to keep our original date. Our daughters ran with the assignment to coordinate the ceremony and rocked it! It was a beautiful day, and the air was filled with love. Our beloved daughters were my bridesmaids, and our handsome grandsons held the honor of being groomsmen.

It was more perfect than anything we could have imagined. We were planning a large celebration, but nothing could compare to our experience under the heavens that day. We felt God's presence all around us, and we knew that He was speaking, leading, guiding, and extending His unconditional love to us. Our love has been redeemed by His amazing grace. We laughed, we cried, and celebrated our love for each other and our family. It was a day we will never forget. We are so grateful for the love and support of our family and friends. We are also grateful for God's grace, which has sustained us through thick and thin. We were excited to start this new chapter in our lives together, and we know that God will continue to bless us.

It takes work to break generational cycles. Sometimes, it takes generations to break them long after we have come into an awareness. Think about it for a moment. Some people may have learned about generational patterns later in life after bringing children into the world. On the other hand, some may have parents or grandparents who were doing the work and breaking these cycles before their children were born. The cycle may have been broken when it reached you. Remember, this is not for everybody, just YOU. Don't look at others and say, "Well, that happened with them," or "Look at so and so" – YOU can only look at your own family lineage. I told you in the beginning that my husband and I both come from large families – there is work to do!

I am grateful today that our beautiful daughters are non-judgmental, loving, kind, generous, and forgiving. More importantly, their struggles have made them stronger, wiser, and encouraged them to establish boundaries. They each have their own journey, and I am proud of the women they are becoming. My prayer for them is an abundance of joy, happiness, good health, and protection.

There are blessings in our lineage. But that is not what we need to overcome. There were many struggles in our lives, as I have stated, and there were many good times as well. If you look deep enough, you will see how blessed your lineage is and also the strong legacy from which you were born. Many people will stop at the blessing because it is too painful to move beyond that to greater abundance. But Jesus said, "I come that you might have life and that life more abundantly" (John 10:10). I encourage you to move beyond your limitations into a life of abundant joy, peace, love, and more than you can imagine.

To be free, we must live in truth. I am transparent about what I felt at that time because emotions can override what we know to be truth in the moment. Sometimes, things don't feel or unfold the way we imagine, but it is not our plan that brings us victory. It is God's plan. All things were working together for our good. We could no longer hold on to the past. Jesus said if you are willing to lose your life, you will gain it. Just when I began to see things differently, the healing began for both of us. Change your thinking and you will eventually change your surroundings. The change had been developing in both of us. God was strengthening our roots through trials and tough decisions, while He was bringing our hearts and minds together on one accord.

And though there are times we feel we failed, God's grace, mercy, and faithfulness lifts us above all the rubble into His marvelous light, giving us the capacity to love more deeply, fully, and compassionately. This time around, we were unlearning the individuals of the past and getting to know each other as new creatures in Christ. Surely, we were not the same people. We felt we knew each other's proclivities, fears, and desires, but we found that we were still reacting to the person of the past in a present-day experience. The truth is, we did not fully trust each other. At times I did not trust the process, but God exposed my heart, and the dismantling began. I heard it said that "sometimes, we're so focused on the future that we don't realize we're in the middle of what we prayed for."

I will not attempt to deceive you into thinking that I have arrived, not in the least. Life is a journey. I am further along the journey of life, but I realize I am not travelling alone. Far be it from me to suggest that my life is perfect and that my husband and I are living in marital bliss. We have challenges, we disagree, we sometimes hurt each other unintentionally, but we are respectful, our convictions are real, and we are committed to our covenant this time around. We have been given a new chapter to rewrite the narrative as dictated by the Author of our faith.

You may be reading this book because you were drawn to the title or supporting a friend. Whether you can relate to my story or desire to marry and raise a family someday, I pray that you will start doing the work today. When we do the healing work, we allow God to show us ourselves, heal, and deliver us from the wounds, judgments, and attitudes (behaviors) of the past. Many people continue the cycle because they have achieved some level of success but never healed. They never realize or accept responsibility for the pain they have caused themselves and others. That within itself is painful. It's easier to say, "This is who I am" and expect others to accept the take-it-or-leave-it attitude. We all sin and fall short of the glory of God. We are not perfect, but that is no longer an excuse. Healing ourselves is necessary if we are to be vessels of healing and compassion in our families, communities, and the world. It does not happen overnight it happens on the journey – if we are willing to humble ourselves.

Everyone has a story and not everyone can relate. However, this story is for the one who desires to be set free for the glory of God! Hallelujah! I believe that God will heal what you are willing to reveal. Exposing the place of your greatest pain allows the Healer to come into your heart, heal those broken places, and restore you to a life of peace and joy!

My blueprint for life is in the Word of God. Over the years I have learned what works for me and offer the same to you:

Prayer and Worship

Talk to God and share your heart with Him. I learned this from my great grandmother. She would sit in her chair by the window and talk to God as if He were sitting in the room with her. Why? Because He *was* sitting in the room with her; He is omnipresent. He promised to never leave us nor forsake us. He says to call upon Him and He will show us great and mighty things we do not know.

Meditation

Focus on God's word and promises. Imagine them both operating in your life and see yourself as a doer of God's Word.

162

Wait and listen for His response to your petition. When God speaks to you through the Holy Spirit, listen and receive His correction and instructions for your life.

Repentance

Repentance is our opportunity to take ownership and responsibility for our sins toward God and man. There are times we need to apologize to others. Follow the unction of the Holy Spirit and obey. Do not justify wrong actions and behaviors. Receive forgiveness and move forward.

Study God's Word

Study the Word of God until it becomes your language. Studying God's Word brings you closer to understanding who God is and His promises. The Word of God is filled with wisdom for your life.

When I reflected on our past relationship, I would say to myself in hindsight, "If I had just been forgiving, if I had been more understanding, if I had held my heart open, if I had known." But now I know, and I would not trade a thing for our journey. **This is our story of Redeeming Love.**

Biography: Deborah Robinson

Deborah Robinson is a real estate professional serving the Richmond, Virginia, and tri-city areas. Deborah began her real estate career in North Carolina in 2005, where she held a real estate sales and broker's license. She holds a B.S. in psychology and an M.A. in law. Deborah facilitates homebuyer workshops and hosts financial literacy events at the community center where she grew up. She also holds a life/health insurance license and Lean Six Sigma certificate in organizational process improvement. She uses her training to provide a holistic approach to educating her clients and community on building generational wealth through home ownership. She is grateful for every opportunity to serve.

Deborah loves studying and sharing the Word of God with others. Her favorite scripture is Proverbs 4:7, *"Wisdom is the principal thing; therefore, get wisdom and with all thy getting get understanding."* She is a strong believer in God's power to heal broken relationships, marriages, and individuals. She is an advocate for the reconciliation and restoration of families. This passion is demonstrated in her calling to rebuild, restore, and renew. She believes that all things are possible through the transformation power of God.

Deborah remarried the love of her life, Torrence Robinson. Together they have two daughters and three grandchildren. She loves spending quality time with her family, reading, listening to music, traveling, and gathering with extended family and friends. She loves God and finds great joy encouraging others to follow their passions.

Deborah Robinson

farmerdd@gmail.com

804-437-1403

Made in the USA
Middletown, DE
11 August 2023

36470937R00099